YES! WE CAN CHANGE INDIA

Abhay

A Common-man

PUSTAK MAHAL®

Publishers
Pustak Mahal®

Administrative office and sale centre

J-3/16 , Daryaganj, New Delhi-110002
☎ 23276539, 23272783, 23272784 • *Fax:* 011-23260518
E-mail: info@pustakmahal.com • *Website:* www.pustakmahal.com

Branches
Bengaluru: ☎ 080-22234025 • *Telefax:* 080-22240209
E-mail: pustakmahalblr@gmail.com
Mumbai: ☎ 022-22010941, 022-22053387
E-mail: unicornbooksmumbai@gmail.com
Patna: ☎ 0612-3294193 • *Telefax:* 0612-2302719
E-mail: rapidexptn@gmail.com

ISBN 978-81-223-1493-9

Edition: 2016

Printed at : AR Emm International, Delhi

Dedication

"To the common men and especially youth of India", with a hope that they will do their best for India to change and develop it.

Contents

To The Reader

I, a common-man, can change India if people of India and especially youths of India listen to my words, and they think, self-analyse and make efforts for it. We have capability to change India but we need all to make effort for it. Without effort of one-and-all, India can never become a developed country.

In my all books, I have written about only one core issue, and that is, how to develop our people and society. How to eradicate poverty, unemployment, illiteracy, injustice and discriminations, and corruption, which are the main obstacles in the development of our people and society—our nation? This subject is so vast and complex that, from the ancient history—from Gautama Buddha to Gandhi, many intelligent and awakened people have thought and worked on it; but still this issue is not resolved. Still, we have not succeeded to change and develop our people and society—our India.

We have proved failure in developing a healthy, balanced and prosperous India. Therefore, at this stage, when we have reached modern science age, we must think and ask ourselves—why we have proved failure in achieving our aim. Why we have failed to develop a healthy, prosperous and developed India. And after a lot of thinking, studying and analysing, I have found that the basic cause behind our failure and underdevelopment is—only a very few people, even less than 5% , have sincerely thought-and-worked for it.

Everyone has not made effort and worked for it. Everyone has not strived for it and hence we could not achieve our aim. And, I can firmly say that until and unless everyone thinks and makes effort for it, we can never change and develop India. No leader, government, guru or god can develop it. Therefore, we must all need to think and make effort to change and develop India; and this responsibility comes especially on the shoulder of youths of India. The youths of India are more innovative, dynamic and energetic, and hence they are capable to take this responsibility. I am also one of youths of India and I took this responsibility and I am doing whatever is possible for me. This book is also a part of this responsibility.

I am grateful to all sources of information which I have used in this book. I am also thankful to all those people who have encouraged and inspired me for writing. Among them, especially, I would like to thank the following dignitaries—Smt. Pratibha Patil, Ex-president of India; Smt. Meena Malla, Director of Lok Sabha Secretariat; Dr. Kiran Bedi, first woman-IPS and well known social activist; Prof. G.. Veerraju, HOD (Philosophy) of Andhra University; Sri I.K. Jha, CWH, Material Organisation, Visakhapatnam—a Unit of Indian Navy (where I also work).

My thanks are due also to Sri GVN Sivanand, a high school English teacher, for his long editorial labour over the manuscript of this book.

I cannot miss to mention the cooperation of my wife Mrs. Priyanka Singh and son Master Vibhav Singh who provided congenial work environment at my home.

Additionally, I feel to express my thanks to all my friends and well wishers who have provided their kind support in publishing this work. I am also thankful to my publisher for materializing this effort elegantly in the present shape. And finally, I am thankful to you, the reader, for picking up this book to read and to give a change in India.

We all need to contribute our part to change and develop India, only then India can change. Your feedback and suggestions are cordially invited at my email.

Abhay
A Common-man
Email: abhay.afriend@gmail.com
Facebook: www.facebook.com/abhay.afriend
Website: www.yeswecanchangeindia.com
Mobile: +91 93463 04747

Disclaimer

In order to maintain the ease of reading, the book uses masculine form of third person throughout this book. This is not to be misinterpreted as being gender biased. The author believes in equality of men and women in every field of life and the book supports the cause.

Foreword

Really it is a great privilege to write a foreword to this book—Yes! We Can Change India. It is the need of time that someone should write such a book, and Mr. Abhay, a common-man—as he has introduced himself in this book, has fulfilled this demand. Today, not only India but even the world is facing such burning issues like poverty, unemployment, population-explosion, illiteracy, hunger, malnutrition, corruption etc. In this breakthrough book, Mr. Abhay has created a platform to discuss these burning issues with a high degree of objectivity. In addition, he has invited all of us to share our views and efforts as well, to change and develop India into a developed nation, which is the dream of all Indians.

This book has been written keeping in mind the youth of India as youth is the key factor in development of India. Youth are vibrant, creative and energetic. More importantly, they are boiling to change India—to change its system, administration and political scenario. It is special in many ways—simple, innovative and practical, and having a touch of science and spirituality. This book covers all social and national issues and awakens us for making effort to change for development. Most importantly, instead of dos and don'ts like most of such books do, this book has been written in a dialogue-manner presenting an open discussion.

It discards all false myths and beliefs about human and social development and puts a real and down-to-earth picture in front of us. For development, it encourages us for putting our best effort and discarded beliefs in luck, fate and destiny. Self-effort and work-with-determination are the basic keys of progress and this book strongly justifies this eternal truth.

I am enthusiastic about the results you will gain in reading this book. Really, it is a gift to the people of India—especially to the youth of India. I strongly recommend everyone to read this book and utilize its thinking for his/ her development and to share his/ her part in the development of India. We can change India only when we will all share our part for it. Jai Hind!

Prof. G. Veerraju,
HOD (Philosophy), Andhra University

1
Poverty and Unemployment
– The Biggest Challenges of India

I think I do not need to present data and reports to see that poverty and unemployment are the biggest problems of our country and even of world. If one has eye-and-heart, one can easily see that at least 40% Indians, means at least 50 crores Indians are facing these problems. These people have not proper employment and income and hence they have not proper food, cloth and shelter. These people are cheap and valueless. Every day they struggle for their survival. They do this-and-that and get some money and fill their stomach to survive. They are living only for namesake without any life.

In my view, poverty and unemployment are so big and critical problems of India that, in front of these two problems, all other problems are very small and tiny. Only because of poverty and unemployment, we have problems like malnutrition, many diseases caused due to malnutrition, hunger, suicide of farmers, child-labour, child-abuse etc. These all problems make our country a bad, dirty and a notorious place. We have to eradicate these problems and youths of India have the maximum role and responsibility in this regard. We have to eradicate poverty in the same manner as we have eradicated polio from India. We have to bring every person above poverty line by providing him employment with a justified salary.

Do We Need to Define Poverty?: Recently, in politics and media, there was a big discussion about poverty and poor people. Some leaders say that a person can have a meal with just ₹5, someone says with ₹12 etc. Experts of Planning Commission and economists define poverty and poverty-line in their own ways. However, I want to say to all these people that if you would take birth in a poor family, you would have better knowledge and experience about poverty. I wish existence may provide you such an opportunity!

Unfortunately, in this life, I get this opportunity and I have a very painful experience of it. This experience is so painful that I never want to experience it again, and therefore I want to eradicate this problem not only from India but even from the world. However, for this, I need help of everyone and especially of youth of India. Only youth of India have power to change this country. No leader, guru, god or government can change India but only you can.

If you want me to define poverty-line, I can define it in a very simple and practical manner: a person, who eats everyday good and nutritious food items like rice, pulses, chapatti, vegetables, fruits and salad, and drinks milk and pure-water and lives in a comfortable house is above poverty-line and remaining people are below poverty-line. Now, you calculate how many people of India are above poverty-line? Your data will be totally changed from the government-data.

Friends, we can clearly see that in India, there are crores of people whose basic needs like food, cloth, shelter and healthcare are not fulfilled. These people are not living but they are dying. They are just waiting for their natural death. In case, if someone could not wait for his natural death, he commits suicide. This is the actual story of poor India, and I myself have gone through this reality of poor India. You will also read my real story in this book.

Therefore, we do not have to define poverty in this way or that way as political leaders and experts of Planning Commission do so. Poverty is a matter of experience with our heart and soul and not a matter of defining with our brain. Poor are in front of us, we have to see them, touch them, feel their difficulties and if possible, do something for them.

Eradicate Unemployment – Poverty Will Be Naturally Eradicated: To change India, we urgently need to eradicate poverty and unemployment. We just need to eradicate unemployment and poverty will be naturally vanished. I was born poor—why, because my father was an unemployed. Though he is a science-graduate but unemployed. And I remained poor until I got an employment. Now, my family is not poor. Also, after marriage, I decided to give birth to only one child thinking that my family could not become poor again. My parents had also done family-planning—only two children; olden way of family-planning—*hum-do-hamaare-do*!

Observing the present position of India, it is clear that we have poverty and unemployment only because of huge population. Due to huge population, people are cheap, they have no value. For one job there are 10,000 eligible candidates—to whom government or private company give that job. Here, I am not talking about big jobs—executive and administrative class of jobs having salary of 6 digits, but I am talking about C and D grade jobs—clerk and labour grade jobs. Poor and common men need these jobs.

Even a salary of C or D grade job is not bad to survive a small family. A couple with one child can easily survive with this salary. I myself am living a peaceful and happy life with this salary. In fact, my present life is many times far better than my past life. In my experience, during poverty, I was not living but slowly dying. I started living only after getting a secured job—a government job in Indian Navy. Poverty was killing me like a slow-poison, but a day came in my life when this poison was vanished.

However, to reach that day, I had to struggle for nearly 4-5 years. In fact, the day when I had joined the government job, I was feeling so happy and relaxed that I consider that day as enlightenment-day of my life! Perhaps, in jungle, one day Siddhartha—the Gautama Buddha had felt the same peacefulness after his continuous effort of 6-7 years. Gautama Buddha was a prince, a wealthy person, so he wanted peace, enlightenment, liberation, God etc. but I was a poor person and therefore I wanted a job and this job gave me the enlightenment-experience.

In India, to solve unemployment problem in a limited period of time, we need at least one crore jobs opportunity every year. Every year, more than 30 lakhs people complete their graduations, and certainly, every graduate is eligible for a C grade job.

However, no leader or political-party can provide these many jobs to youths of India. We may select any political party—Congress, BJP, Third-front, Left, Right etc. (here, I cannot mention nan es of all political parties of India as I need a paragraph to mention all of them and it is wastage of paper and time)—means, from all over India, we may select and elect any leader and political party, but no leader and political-party can provide these many jobs to us. In fact, in this matter to put the reality, I want to say that, even all intelligent leaders of world cannot do this job for India, what to say about our Indian leaders. You know how much they are intelligent and capable—and cunning and corrupt as well!

So, we, the common men and especially youths of India, must think ourselves (as I think) what we can do to solve poverty and unemployment problems and how we can change the future of our country.

Family-Planning – The Only Way: Friends, without population control, one third population of India will be always poor and unemployed. We have to raise every person above poverty-line, and for that, we need to give employment (with a justified-salary) to everyone. However, due to huge population and crores of unemployed people, we have left only one way—we urgently need population control and for that we need family-planning. In this matter, we need to follow China-policy, that is—one or no one. Otherwise, if we want a little flexibility, we can produce two children, but more than two—we should never think about that. Also, sometime a twin may take birth, so we need a little flexibility! With the same thinking, I have also given birth to only one child.

Our government should urgently make a law that a couple cannot have more than two children—'Maximum Two' policy. Actually, for population control, what prime-minister Indira Gandhi had started doing nearly four decades back, present government and leaders need to do the same thing. After independence, if we could have controlled our population, the condition of poor-Indians had not been this much deteriorated. Government and leaders must think rising above vote-bank politics, only then we can solve our root-level problems; otherwise, century-after-century, we will face these problems. No God will come to solve these problems. I am saying this because some people are waiting for a God to come and solve these problems. Your wait and prayer will be proved futile. So, we ourselves have to think and make effort to solve our problems.

Why Do We Give Birth to Our Children?: The difficulties and problems of India show that most of the people are very irresponsible towards caring and development of their children. People have produced their children to fulfill their own selfish desires and not to develop them. Poor people want children as they need helpers and extra hands and rich people want children as they need successor of their wealth and multi-million-empire. This is the actual psychology of most of the people behind giving birth to their children.

Both rich and poor people have spoiled their children and consequently they have spoiled society and humanity. Besides, rich people have no care and concern for the poor people, and sadly poor people have no care for even their children. Poor people give birth to their children and simply leave them to survive on their fate and destiny. What a tragedy of humanity!

From thousands of years, our religions and spirituality have taught us that human-world is like a joint-family. We are brothers, sisters and friends, and we should help each other in our development. But in practical, we are just selfish and self-centered and nothing more. In our relations, everything starts and ends with self, and its adverse result is in front of us—huge population, poverty, unemployment, pollution, diseases, hunger, misery, and downtrodden lives of millions of people. Now, we should stop this situation from becoming more critical and deteriorated, and it is possible only by family planning so that every couple can care and develop his children in a proper manner. Our children are our future and we must care our future.

Please Don't Give Poverty to Your Child: Dear common men, you may be surprised to hear it, but it is a fact that government and ministers are not giving poverty to our children but we are giving it to them; how? Because, we know very well that government and ministers have been proved failure in eradication of poverty of our parents, grand-parents and ourselves. So before giving birth to our children, we must think that the same government and ministers will also be proved failure in eradication of poverty of our children? Today, if more than 50 crores people of India are poor, it is only because we have not thought about this point. We have not taken care of future of our children. We simply hoped that government and ministers would eradicate our poverty, but ultimately our hope proved futile. So, if we want to eradicate poverty of our children, we must care this point before giving birth to them.

You know what I usually say to my 12 years old child; I usually tell him, if you could be able to get a job, you marry a girl, otherwise don't marry. And in case, if you would be interested to marry a girl, you marry but remain childless! Do not give poverty to your child by-birth and extra-burden on your parents. I am saying this because you are not very interested in studies and without studies a common man cannot get a job.

Of course, I know talking to a 12 years old child in this manner seems absurd, but I must say to every common man and especially youth of India that if we want to change and develop India, we must stop giving born-poverty to our child. First arrange basic needs of your child and then give birth to him, otherwise be childless. Please leave this outdated logic that God gives birth to a child and not we. Before giving this logic, first meet God and confirm this matter with Him. Don't believe gurus and spiritual teachers. Most of them are talking useless and nonsense things. So, don't think blindly this and that about God. Leave all outdated beliefs and stories about God.

From practical observation of living world, it is clear that only an animal like a cat or dog gives birth to his kids without arranging basic needs for their kids. So, if you think you are a man and not an animal—live like a man and arrange basic needs for your kids. In addition, I say to people of India that to fulfill our basic needs, do not depend on government and God—no luck, fate and destiny; no free and cheap rasan, no mid-day meals for kids—nothing free. From government we should ask for employment with a justified-salary and not free or cheap rasan and mid-day meals. We must leave our free-and-cheap mentality, only then we can save our children from poverty, unemployment, child labour and child abuse; and consequently we can change India into a developed country.

Government Should Make People Empowered and Not Dependent: Before making policies and schemes, government and leaders must think that they should not make people slave and dependent on them. Government should make people empowered. Polices and schemes that make people dependent on government lead people away from empowerment. In this regard, someone has rightly said—you give a man fish, you feed him a day; you teach him how to fish you feed him for a life time. Surely, such teachings, trainings and developing-skills take time, but we need to give them such teachings, trainings and skills. So, policies have to be well thought out and have right intention.

Policies only for short-sighted political gain will lead this country to hell. 40% people of India are already in hell; at least, we should make effort to bring their children out of this hell. I know it is a difficult task, but if our thinking and intention is good, certainly we can complete this task in a limited period of time. If a common man like me can think and make effort for it, you intelligent and powerful leaders must think and make effort for it.

We Need All to Think-and-Work to Solve Our Problems: Really, India is such a country which is difficult to define and describe. Can we say India is a poor country because

India has many top-level rich people? In my own joint family, there was a millionaire, but remaining people were poor and ordinary and my parents were one of them. Can we say India is an underdeveloped country—because we are developed in every field of development? We can stand in front of any country in any field. However, on ground level, it is a fact that today—at least, 50 crores Indians are poor and unemployed. They are illiterate, unhealthy, cheap and downtrodden. Apart from this, at present, we are facing problems like—high-inflation, low growth rate of economy, no infrastructure for development, scams and corruption, hatred and violence in the name of caste, class, religion etc.

Really, the condition of India is very critical and common men are in an abominable condition. But what is the way to come out of this drastic and abominable situation—we all have to think. Only government and leaders cannot bring us out from this abominable condition. Only changing leaders and government from Congress to BJP or Third-front to Forth-front is not going to solve our problems.

Do you know, till now I have never voted for any leader or party? I do not know whom to vote—who is good and who is bad. Also, I am not interested to read other's bio-data and biography so that I may be able to know about him in a better way. In exception, I have read Mahatma Gandhi's biography. Really he is a great-ordinary man! I have great respect for this common man and his biography is simply fantastic. I do not find any other biography so real and genuine. In fact, most of such books are fake and showy like our fake leaders and politicians.

As we know, every party has some good as well as some cunning and corrupt people; otherwise, you and especially CBI suggest me which party has every person good and sincere, I will vote for that party! I know you cannot suggest me. And therefore, I have kept myself aside of all leaders and parties. Even I meet a leader or a minister (as you can see me meeting Mrs. Sheila Dikshit, Ex-CM of Delhi, at the end of this book), I meet him to present my book with a kind request for his compliments. However, here I would like to mention that it is really a difficult task for a common man to meet our leaders and ministers. We select them to listen to our difficulties and to solve them but they have no time and interest to listen to our difficulties. They are real VIPs with power, properties and prestige (3Ps). In present age, these 3Ps—power, properties and prestige, define a person as VIP and not his virtue, talent and intelligence.

Anyway, we should understand that leaders and ministers are also human beings like us. They have no special talent and intelligence to solve our problems in a magical way. They are as ordinary and normal human beings as we are. God has not created much difference among us. More importantly, if people like Gautama Buddha and Mahatma Gandhi say that they are common-man and not special and great, then definitely we are all same—a common man. Certainly, present leaders and politicians have money, power, status and security. We cannot touch them; we cannot go even close to them. But this type of power, status and security cannot solve our problems; no, never. So, only our work and efforts with understanding can solve our problems.

Therefore, we should all think and work-out our thinking to come-out of our problems. Just thinking is not enough; we also need to work-out our thinking. There have been many thinkers in India and the world. So, we do not need thinkers anymore. We need only workers now. I know most of the people want to become leaders and ministers, but friends; we should understand that if everyone will become a leader and minister, then who will work on the ground. If everyone will give ideas and directions, then who will follow those ideas and directions—in that situation, we will all be confused. So, let only intelligent, awakened and IAS-ranked people guide us, and remaining people work on the ground. And, please do not consider me an author or thinker, as I am a worker at ground level—I work in Indian Navy as a common employee. It is other matter that I feel to say something to common people considering them as friends, and I started writing. So, I am a common man like most of the common men of India, but like actor Shahrukh Khan—Chennai Express, I must say, "Don't underestimate the power of a common man!"

We Need Help and Support from Every Person: For development, everyone has to think and work. Even the commonest of the common man and the poorest of the poor man has to think and work. Every person has to give his best support. If you cannot do great things, no problem, do small things like give birth to only one child, make proper arrangement for growth of your child, give him nutritious food, send him to school, teach him daily one hour at home etc. There are many such small things that every person can do like switch-off light, fan and TV when they are not in use; keep your surroundings clean; plant trees; teach poor children etc. These small things can make a big difference.

If you simply blame and be-depended on God and government; then nothing is going to change. You will be always poor and downtrodden. You will spoil your life and also life of your family and children. So, you must think 'what you can do for yourself and your family—and if possible, for others—for society and humanity, for India and world.' Of course, first you think and act for yourself—arrange basic needs of your life and get whatever you want to enjoy your life—after that, think-and-act for others. I am fully agreed with Chetan Bhagat's "Sparks"—'love yourself first, and then others'. I have done same thing in my life. First, I have arranged basic needs for myself and my family and then I have thought about others.

Only in a story, and especially in a holy and religious story, a person keeps himself starved and feeds others. We have many such olden holy and religious stories in our scriptures but of no use. Children read such holy stories in their childhood and forget them when they grow adult. They become practical. Now, for them honesty does not matter but success matters—success in money, power and status. So, young generation is practical and if we want change and development, we must be practical. Only theory and emotional story cannot change and develop us. They cannot provide us employment and solve our root level problems. Therefore, the commonest of the common man must think-and-work to solve his problems.

Only Education Cannot Change India—How and Why?: Though illiteracy is a big obstacle in development of our country, the main obstacle is lack of simple logic and reasoning power in common men. People are not practical. They are selfish, ignorant and short-sighted. They know only how to blame others for their problems. They blame parents, family, friends, society, leaders, government, God, fate and destiny—in fact, everyone except themselves. In their eyes, for their problems, everyone is blamable except themselves. This is the position of most of the common men.

To prove how education is ineffective in our development, here I have mentioned a ground reality of our people. Educated people definitely know that huge population is the basic cause of our poverty and unemployment. Even a third-standard student knows that a small family is a happy family. Big family and many children make us poor. However, in India, even graduates have produced more than four children. Even some of graduate leaders have not thought about this matter. Some of them have produced more than half a dozen of children. Such is our people, society and country. From 33 crores in 1947, we become 120 crores in 2013.

Why people have done so—very simple; because, through education, they have become knowledgeable but their thinking, sensibility and awareness have not been developed. They have memorized facts and data of books and have got degrees and jobs—most of them not, but this mental-exercise has not developed their thinking and awareness. Otherwise, how a knowledgeable and sensible person can produce more than two children?

After getting independence of India, if we had just controlled our population, the condition of poor-Indians had not been this much deteriorated. At that time, we were poorer than present-India. British government had raped and crushed us like anything. So, after independence, if we had controlled population, India had become a developed and prosperous country now. But, about our past, what is the use of weeping and crying—nothing. I am also not interested in our past. I am interested only in present, in now; because whatever we have to do we have to do it now. And therefore, I want to talk mostly youth of India because they think in a do-it-now manner.

Only because of ignorance and lack of simple reasoning-power, people have accepted so many myths and beliefs as realities—like beliefs in luck, fate and destiny, beliefs in lines of hands and head, beliefs in stars and planets. These myths and beliefs have created many problems in their life. Due to these very beliefs, most of the people have given birth to many children. They have produced child-after-child and have left them on their fate and destiny. They have left them to-die or remain-alive on their fate and destiny. If a child dies, they simply think—it is the fault of child's fate and God and not theirs. Such is the poor belief-system of our people. With such a poor belief-system how we can develop India; no we can't. Therefore, we must leave this poor belief-system, and we should all think what we can do for India, only then we can develop a healthy and prosperous India. Besides, if you cannot do anything for India, just do one thing, a little thing—give birth to only one child. This little thing can create a big difference in India.

Poverty—Religious and Spiritual View: India is a spiritual country. About religion and spirituality, India talks more than any other countries in the world. India is also famous as world-guru! However, it is world-guru only for namesake. Reality is that it has been never a world-guru—neither in past nor in present. Surely, India has produced people of world-guru caliber like Sri Krishna, Gautama Buddha, Mahavira, Guru Nanak, Kabir etc. But just by giving birth to such people a country does not become a world-guru. A country becomes world-guru with progress and development and we have to achieve that development by our work and effort.

Since India is a religious and spiritual country, so here I would also like to talk about poverty from a religious and spiritual point of view so that people may be aware of the ground reality from all points of view. Spirituality says that any person, who is greedy and hungry, is a poor. Even a millionaire, who is greedy for money is a poor. I am fully agreed with this spiritual view. There are many people in this country and even in the world, who have everything to live a comfortable, peaceful and happy life, but they are not happy and satisfied. They want more—more and more—unlimited. For these people, only inner-peace and inner-awakening can give some solution and nothing else.

Before becoming a Buddha, Siddhartha—a wealthy man, a prince, was in the same situation. Only after increasing his inner-peace and inner-awakening, he became peaceful and enlightened. So, such type of poverty is an individual's problem and not a social or national problem. If you are interested to read this type of poverty, you better read my book—How to Develop One and All, which is freely available on my website: www.yeswecanchangeindia.com. In this way, we need not printing of books and we can save our trees and environment.

Friends, truly speaking, religion and spirituality cannot eradicate poverty and unemployment from our country. For this, only work and efforts with understanding can help us. Such things advertised on TV like Shubh Dhan-Varsha (advertised by actor Govinda) and other religious and spiritual devices and techniques cannot finish our poverty. They cannot give us money and prosperity. And what a contradiction we see—an actor, who is advertising for Shubh Dhan-Varsha, is acting as a thief in cinema—Loot! Why are you acting as a thief and giving a wrong message to our society. Just keep 3-4 Shubh Dhan-Varsha in your home and wealth will start raining on you!

Friends, unless we understand the root causes of our problems and make efforts to remove them, even God—our Creator cannot help us; what to say a hero or a leader, or a guru or a god! No, no one can help us. All such people do their business in the name of helping us. A hero gives us fun and entertainment and in returns he earns crores of rupees, a guru or god delivers a holy lecture and in returns he enjoys a luxurious life, and a leader gives us attractive speech and assurance and in returns he gets our votes and hence power and money. So, please do not be trapped in such goody-goody advertisements and fake-assurances. Think, understand and work-hard to solve your problems.

I Want To Meet God Now!: Once I had gone to a spiritual institution. (Intentionally, I don't want to mention its name and place. In fact, in my writing, I do not want to mention anything which may create animosity and hatred in common people and society. I want to change India not with violence, strike, and bloody-revolution, but with awareness, sensibility, love, friendliness and cooperation.) At that time, I was nearly 19 years old and I was struggling to get a job.

At the spiritual institution, as usual, a spiritual guru was delivering a beautiful goody-goody holy speech about God. I heard him for few minutes and only within few minutes, I was so irritated with his goody-goody speech that I asked him abruptly, "Where is God, I want to meet him now?" He replied, "You come here for one week, I will show you God."

I asked, "Why after one week, why not now? Whether your God is sleeping now and you do not want to disturb Him? If you can show Him now, show me now, otherwise I can't wait for Him for one week. I haven't that much time to spare for meeting God! I have other jobs and the most important job is studies to get a job. For me, getting a job is more important than meeting God. Moreover, I want to say that if I meet God, the first thing I will ask Him is a job for me. So, I want to know from you that can your God provide me a job. I need a job to come out of my poverty. So, can your goody-goody great God arrange a job for me? And by the way, why only for me, if He is great and merciful and He has power to do everything, then He can easily arrange a job for everyone. We are all His children and He should care all of us."

For a few moments, the spiritual guru was answerless and then he started usual stories—this-and-that, ifs and buts, shoulds and shouldn'ts etc. I interrupted him in the middle and said, "I don't want such usual stories, I have read lots of such usual stories in spiritual and religious books. So, please don't repeat them again here. Just tell only one thing that can your God arrange a job for me or not—'Yes' or 'No'.

Again for a few moments, he was voiceless and then started stories… and our argument might have been continued further, if in the mean time one of the institution's members had not come and interrupted it. After this incident, I had never gone there to waste my time in useless argument. So, friends, just by listening to goody-goody views and stories about God, our problems cannot be solved. They can be solved only by hard work and efforts with understanding and sensibility.

I Accept Only That God—Who… : People believe that God makes us rich and poor. However, I can never accept such a God who makes someone rich or poor as per His (God's) wish and will. I accept only that God, who gives fruits of our work and effort, and I know such a God and that God is this Existence, this universe. Yes, this existence is our real God—our Creator.

We have been created and nurtured by this existence. Our God is in front of us and not hidden somewhere in the sky. It is only our ignorance due to which we think and pray an alien-God. Be aware that our God is made up of atoms and energies and its every atom and energy-particle is in motion and action at every moment. These particles, through their motions and actions, give us this clear message that we should also move and work like them.

We should work to fulfill our needs and desires. Simply sitting and believing in luck, fate and destiny is not going to fulfill our needs and desires. There is no God in the whole of universe who writes our fate and destiny. Such a God and His concept of fate and destiny are just illusions created by religion and spirituality to give us false consolation.

In fact, here I have explained the same olden philosophy of karma which thousands of years back Lord Sri Krishna had explained in Bhagawad Gita—Karmanye Vadhikaraste, Ma phaleshou kada chana… Really, it is matter of shame for us that a country, where a person like Lord Sri Krishna had been born, is in such a poor and downtrodden condition. It is matter of shame that a country that had Gita from thousands of years, remained slave for thousands of years.

It shows that in spiritual knowledge, we are not world-guru but a parrot-guru! We know only to speak like a parrot, but do not know how-to-live and how-to-war according to our spirituality. Seeing all this, the soul of Lord Sri Krishna must be annoying and crying somewhere in space. I think He is very much annoyed from us and therefore he is not taking birth again, as he had declared thousands of years back—Yada Yada Hi Dharmasya... He has left us alone to think and decide ourselves so that we may become strong and self-dependent.

Now we have to use our inherent-spiritual power and experience to prove that we are not parrot-guru but the real world-guru. Only then we can change India and we will prove that we are the children of people like Lord Sri Krishna and Gautama Buddha.

If someone is not agreed with my views about God, I would like to say him that bring that God 'alive' in front of me in which you believe in. I will discuss this issue with Him and make it clear. In fact, I discuss such issues with the real God, that is—the creator existence, so I can definitely discuss such issues with any guru, god, leader or scientist born on this earth or anywhere in the universe!

So, please stop simply wishing and praying God. No, this way, God is not going to help us. He is not going to fulfill our wish. You make efforts and strive for your goal; God will definitely try to fulfill your wish. Someone has rightly said—God helps those who help themselves. And be clear that God also tries—God has not any magic-wand—simply moved and your wish is fulfilled. No, it has been never happened on this earth. Only in religious stories, our God has magic-wand otherwise the real-God has not any magic-wand. God has power and potential to work, to make efforts.

I repeat that God is made-up of atoms and energy-particles, and its every particle is working day-and-night continuously. So we should also work to reach our goal and solve our problems. (As a matter of fact, I am not agreed with modern scientists who say that God-particle is only one—Higgs Boson, which they have discovered recently after a huge-experiment of long-years. As per my experience, every particle is a God-particle—atom, energy, electron, proton, neutron, neutrino etc.; all are God's particles. In fact, not only these particles, but we are also God-particles! Every human being is a God-particle. So, make your view clear and broader.) Therefore, we have left only one way to fulfill our desire and solve our problems, and that is, make effort with understanding and sensibility.

God Does Not Make Anyone Poor: As we believe that everything has been predetermined and prewritten in our fate and destiny, and no one can change our fate and destiny. Friend, if you think that God has made you poor and downtrodden, then I suggest you to discard that God! Actually, you not only discard that God but also hate Him! I myself have discarded and hated that God in my childhood and youth.

Even today, I hate such a God who makes a man poor as per His own wish. He (God) does not care work and efforts of a person and simply does whatever He (God) likes. In this life, I am also a born-poor and people used to say me the same old-stories about God. I left all such stories of gods and goddesses and also—their blessings, their wills and wishes, and their planning of luck, fate and destiny. In my very teenage, I had said to all gods and goddesses that what you have written in my destiny—I don't know and I don't care, because I will write my destiny with my own hand—with my own work and effort. And I suggest the same thing to you—especially to the young Indians.

You write your destiny with your own hand—with your own work and effort. Fail or pass—don't bother; you just make effort to your level best. I don't say—nothing is impossible, but I must say—make possible what is possible. And I do say, eradication of illiteracy, poverty and unemployment is totally in our hand and we must make it possible.

Love God Only When You Feel God Loves You: Most of the people love and pray God because they fear of God. They fear that if they will not pray God, God will make harm to them. However, this is a totally wrong and ridiculous thinking. I say, you love God only when you feel God loves you—otherwise do not love God! First, a parent should love and care his child, only then his child can love him. Follow the same thinking with God. I have followed the same thinking in my life.

I started loving God only when I felt that God loves me; He cares me and it took nearly 23 years for me. Since it took nearly 23 years to come out of my poverty—my depressed and dying life. Only after coming out of my poverty, I felt that God loves me. Certainly, during poverty also, I had felt His love and care, but I had not cared of His love. During that period, I had mostly hated and discarded Him! But, the day when I felt His love, there were tears in my eyes and I had said, "You have always loved and cared me and it is only I who have ignored your love and care. I am sorry. Please forgive me."

Therefore friends, we need to change our thinking and belief about God. Never think that God makes us poor, weak, disabled, diseased, handicapped, downtrodden etc. No, never. If God does such bad and evil things, then why we should love such a bad and evil God? No, we should stop loving such an evil God. We should always love a good, caring and loving God and I must say that we have such a caring and loving God and that is Existence.

Our nature, earth, sun, solar-system, and milky-way—these are all tiny parts of our God. So, with my own experience, I want to say rather declare that God does not make anyone poor or weak. God makes everyone intelligent and prosperous and we have to prove it by our work and effort. Praying and worship of God cannot make us intelligent and prosperous—no, never. In fact, our real God says—your work is my worship. Do not pray with your mind and hands but work with them. I have given them to work and not for praying and begging from me or from anyone. So, be sensible and do work, result will certainly come.

Rich Men, Please Don't Misguide Common-Men: Some wealthy and successful people like big businessmen, sport and film stars, political leaders, authors and VIPs say and indirectly advise that their luck, fate and destiny have played a great role in their achievements and success. (Even Chetan Bhagat has written about destiny-concept regarding his achievements and success in his book 'What Young India Wants', but I am totally disagreed with his concept of destiny). This fate and destiny belief which has become thinking-and-attitude of common people creates pseudo-satisfaction in them.

Common people think that they are poor and unsuccessful because their fate and destiny is poor and weak. God has not written their fate and destiny good and great and hence they are poor. They think that their poverty and misery are not their fault but it is the fault of God and His planning. So, for their poverty and misery, God is guilty and blamable and not they are.

What a misery of these people! Already they are poor and ignorant and these pseudo-successful people are helping them to remain poor and ignorant. Already they have cancer and these pseudo-successful people are inserting HIV-virus in them! These pseudo-successful people are advising them that in whatever manner they are thinking and living is right. There is no need to change in their thinking and living. And, I am saying these VIPs and successful people as pseudo-successful because if they are real successful, then what people like Gandhi and Gautama Buddha should be called?

A person like Gandhi is successful or a film-star and a cricketer are successful? So, people like Gandhi and Gautama Buddha are real successful people. Only a person, who works for development of people and society, is a real Hero or a successful person. He or she may belong to any field, but this should be the basic criteria to define a real Hero or a successful person.

Friends, whoever is saying that prosperity and poverty, and success and failure are a matter of fate and destiny, is a guilty in the eye of God—the Creator. He or she may be anyone—a hero, celebrity, star, author, thinker, philosopher, scientist, VIP, leader, guru, god or anyone. Understand that such a person is not a friend of people and humanity, as such a person does not want to develop the whole society and humanity—one and all. He or she wants only self-success. He wants remaining people to see him as a role model, hero and a leader. So, open your third-eye—your wisdom and consciousness, and observe the reality and absorb the truth. Your soul has been burdened with many illogical and absurd beliefs. You have to remove these false beliefs to enlighten your soul.

A person, who blames his fate and destiny for his poverty, failure and misery, he may be a God-believer and devotee but certainly he is not a God-lover. How such a person can be called a God-lover who blames God for his failure and misery; no, he can't be. So, on this earth, only a few people (may be less than 5%) are true God-lovers, remaining are God-believers and God-blamers!

Understand that not only poor and ordinary people are God-blamers but many rich and successful people are also God-blamers. Such rich and successful people blame God because they think that they have not yet achieved their desired goal and success—may be the chair of PM or President, or Bharat-Ratna or Nobel Prize or whatever it may be—*bade logon ki badi baatein*! They think that their planet, star, fate and destiny are not in their favour, and for this, only God and His planning can be blamed and nothing else.

I would like to say rich and successful people that, friends, if you have earned success and prosperity with your talent and hard-work; then you speak out the reality. You say that you have earned it with your talent and hard-work. But please do not bring God in your success-story. Don't say that you are lucky and fortunate. Because, by saying so, indirectly you are blaming God for misery and poverty of billions of people.

Of course, in your own way, you are praising and flattering God, but in the other way, you are proving God a biased and an unfair body. Because, suppose, if someone asks you—who has made poor, ordinary and failure people? What will be your answer? Could you say—God has made poor and failure people? You couldn't say, and in fact, you can never say, because by saying so, you will annoy God, which you can never do. So, in place of saying this, you would say—poor and failure people are poor and failure because they are lazy and stupid. It means you are successful because you are hard-working and intelligent—and this is the right answer.

So, speak-out the reality, otherwise speak in such a manner that your words may awaken others. Your words should give "sparks" to others like the "Sparks" of Chetan Bhagat. First I had read Chetan's "Sparks" in my office (someone has e-mailed it to my officer and I had read it), and after that I had bought his book—What Young India Wants, to read. Before that, I had never studied his any title. I have read many novels and stories in my teenage, so I am not interested in such fictions and stories. I am interested only in reality which has "sparks", so that by reading it, I may enlighten my inner-spark. On this earth, from Gautama Buddha to Rajneesh (OSHO), many "Sparking Souls" have been born in India and the world. In fact, India has produced better "Sparking Souls" in the world.

Seeing this, India may be called as producers of "Sparking Soul" or world-gurus, but we cannot say India—as a whole, a world-guru. To prove India a world-guru, India should be developed in every field and its root-level problems like illiteracy, poverty, unemployment, population-explosion, pollution, corruption etc. must be finished. So, we—especially youth of India need a lot of work to do on personal, social and national basis to prove India a world guru. And I strongly feel that we have capability to change India, we just need electrifying our inner-sparks and this book is for the same purpose.

I know that common people see rich, successful and glamorous people as their role model and Hero. They see Shahrukh, Sachin and Mukesh Ambani as their role models and not people like Abdul Kalam and Anna Hazare. Therefore, I request these rich, glamorous and successful people that you help common people in removing false-belief of luck, fate and destiny. You motivate them for making effort and work-with-sincerity—*dil se*. Finally, I must say belief in luck, fate and destiny is a big hurdle in development of India. We must leave this false belief. Even we need to leave God we can leave God but we must leave this fate and destiny attitude—only then we can change India.

Millionaires! Be Prepared To Become a Slumdog-Millionaire!: In a friendly manner, I would like to say all rich people that today you are millionaires but tomorrow you may also become a born-slumdog! So, be prepared to face the challenges that a slumdog faces. Until there remains a single slumdog on this earth, there is a danger for everyone to take birth as a slumdog. This existence provides opportunity to everyone for development and it is possible only by mixing-up us. Our creator mixes us like the electrons of different energies of an atom—called hybridization in chemistry. We are all children of creator-existence and it takes care of us equally. It has no partiality and biasness.

Understand that if God can give birth to good people like Kabir and Kalam, and Edison and Einstein in poor and ordinary family, then who is safe from poverty—no one. Therefore, Millionaires! You must think-and-act for development of total

India. Not a single person should be left poor in India. And if you want to be 100% safe from poverty then not a single person should left poor in total humanity.

In fact, due to positive-thinking attitude (this attitude is very high in present stressful life), rich people can never think about becoming a poor or a slumdog. They always think about getting more and more power, money and status. But this existence has a different mechanism to work and it does not follow our positive-thinking or rich-become-richer concept; instead it works for development of total humanity—one-and-all. And hence, even a millionaire may have to take birth as a slumdog. He may have to face difficulties and problems of a slumdog.

Certainly, if he is really a talented and intelligent person and he is millionaire because of his talent and intelligence, then he will come out of his downtrodden slumdog-life. Otherwise if he has become millionaire because of his cunningness and corruptness, he will die living a slumdog life.

I know modern people do not believe in soul and life-after-death. And therefore, I challenge modern science to prove me wrong what I am saying with my self-experience above; yes... I am talking about rebirth and immortality of soul—about which Lord Sri Krishna had taught humanity thousands of years back.

I challenge modern science to prove that a man is just a mixture of two sex-cells. Prove that parents are the actual creator of their children. Prove that there is no linkage between past and present life of a human being. Prove that there is no hidden chemistry working behind growth of a man—which is yet to be discovered by modern science. Prove that after death, everything of a human being is destroyed—nothing remains alive. I challenge, you can never prove me wrong and if you can prove me wrong, you can hang me! Are you ready to take my challenge?

Millionaires! Wait For Soul-Transplant!: Though modern medical science knows about organ-transplantation, it has not yet invented any mechanism for soul-transplantation. In fact, it has not even idea about soul—as it has not yet added this word 'soul' in its dictionary. So there is no question of thinking about soul-transplantation. Again, science finds that our brain-cells are not replicated. It means, no died brain-cell is replaced by another one. Once a brain-cell died means it died forever. Therefore, our brain is dying day by day, and consequently, one day it will die completely; and in medical-science terms, brain-death means total-death.

So, our death is certain. However, some optimistic people—and especially rich and billionaire people may hope that one day in future, science may invent a mechanism which may make them immortal—immortal means, permanent-alive in their same body. And really, that will be a great achievement of modern science. But we do not know when science will invent this mechanism.

Therefore, I want to say rich people that until science invents such a mechanism, please stop accumulating more and more wealth with you; because through life-cycle mechanism, the existence will capture your huge wealth and it may give you birth in a poor family making you a born-slumdog. And, in a movie like Slumdog Millionaire, a slumdog easily becomes a millionaire, but in real life, rarely a slumdog becomes a millionaire. One in millions of slumdogs—having a talented and intelligent soul, becomes a millionaire; remaining all slumdogs live as slumdogs and die as slumdogs.

So, you ask yourself—are you capable of becoming a slumdog-millionaire? A couple will give you birth and leave you in a dustbin or somewhere on a road and from there you have to become a millionaire; are you capable of it? If you are capable, you are fit for this world. Present competitive-world needs people like you. But, if you are not capable of it—you are really in danger; and if you want to come out of this danger, help poor and slumdogs to come out of their poverty and downtrodden lives.

Why do I want to finish poverty from India and this world—because I myself feel this danger for me? In my present life, I have felt the pain and misery of poverty. It is really very painful and frustrating. You know only because of poverty I have seen my mother trying to commit suicide. Really I could never face poverty again, and therefore I want to finish it completely from the earth. But, poverty is a big problem and without help and support of one and all, this problem can never be eradicated by me or by anyone—even by God.

I know God very well—He needs our help. In fact, God is crying for our help but we are too busy to listen to His voice. I listen to Him as I am not a busy-man! Business-men are generally busy men and today we have all become business men—always thinking and moving here and there for making money. We should leave this business-thinking and listen to God's voice—our inner-voice, and we should all make effort to eradicate poverty from this earth.

Further, if you think that soul and life-cycle mechanism are just spiritual and religious phony beliefs, and there is no reality in such beliefs, then in my view, first you confirm this matter. Tell modern medical science and all Nobel-prize winner scientists to verify this matter. In fact, to verify and confirm the same matter, one day Siddhartha—the Gautama

Buddha had left his kingdom. He had deep curiosity about this matter and hence he left everything so that he could concentrate his total inner-awareness and experience to find the truth hidden behind this matter.

Therefore, for you, there are three options to confirm this matter: first option, you yourself make effort to clear your doubt like prince Siddhartha. Second option, let science find the truth for you—that is, there is nothing like soul in our body. Soul is just a myth; there is no reality in it. And third option, let science make you immortal in your same body so that you may always remain a millionaire. Otherwise, in one-life you become a millionaire and in another-life you become a slumdog and continue your life-cycle in this manner.

Next, even you earn and accumulate billions of currencies; you could never be able to experience the reality of life-cycle, because if it had been possible, why prince Siddhartha had left his kingdom. Hence, every money-minded and rich person should ask this question to oneself that why Siddhartha had left his kingdom? Think and ponder over this question—you will feel a shake within you and this shake will awaken your inner-conscience. I am sure when you will be able to experience the reality of life-science; you will naturally stop accumulating huge wealth with you. You will start helping others what Siddhartha had done after experiencing the truth.

Poverty Prevents Creativity and Hence Development: Due to poverty, a person thinks day-and-night only about making an arrangement for his bread and butter. Such a person rarely thinks about emerging his art and virtue, and that is why many such poor people die in poverty without emerging their art and virtue. The same thing has been happened in my life. After getting employment,

I settled in my life, and thereafter I became capable of emerging my inner virtue, I started writing for human and social development. Before getting employment, this virtue was hidden within me in a seed form. I have often felt the potential of this seed, because due to this very seed, I have discarded many mythological and religious beliefs in my very young age. Such beliefs and stories seemed very phony and illogical.

Apart from this, while reading books of world famous personalities like religious and spiritual gurus, social reformers, leaders, intellectuals, philosophers, authors, and even of gods, my inner-awareness conveyed me this message that I can explain their views in a somewhat more practical way—or at least, I can add something in their views. However, before getting employment, I could never think about writing a book. But, after getting a secured-employment, within a month, I decided to convey my messages and I started writing. This clearly shows that, for a person, poverty creates a big hindrance in emerging his art and virtue, and if such a person does not come out of poverty we lose his art and virtue which may be proved very useful for development of humanity. Therefore, we must make effort to provide employment (with a justified salary) to every poor man so that we could not lose his art and virtue.

Our All Development Is Zero If We Cannot Eradicate Poverty: If we cannot provide employment to everyone and raise every individual above poverty-line—all leadership, governance, policies and schemes, Planning-commission, Vision-20-20, development, progress, philosophy, religion, spirituality, fashion, modernity, and even science and technology are bogus and absurd. I want to ask what science and technology is doing? Scientists are interested to find what is there on the Moon and Mars? What is there out of our solar-system and galaxy? Is there any life apart from earth or not? But what is the value of all these activities? I do not see any value in them.

Our earth and humanity are in danger and we are wondering here and there in space, why? Our earth is the most beautiful planet in our solar-system and galaxy, and may be in the whole universe, then why we are wondering here and there. Make our earth more beautiful and healthy. For it, control population and pollution, eradicate illiteracy, poverty and unemployment. Making our earth more beautiful should be the first duty and responsibility of science and every intelligent and sensible person. Remember, if we will not solve the root-level problems of our earth, we must pay for its cost and science very well know this cost—I need not to mention it.

2

Corruption
– Cause, Concern and Cure

Corruption- Corruption–Everywhere!

I have faced the same government-offices, and police and administrative departments that other common men generally face and I have same experience what a common man experiences while dealing with these people. A common man does not go on a hunger-strike like Mr. Anna Hazare to fight injustice, discrimination and corruption. A common man simply requests or compromises with government-officials. I think, these are common or general experiences, so I need not to share my experiences in details.

Corruption is everywhere. Corruption is in politics, police-department, judiciary-department, government offices, media, and even at religious and spiritual places. If you find a place without corruption then I think it cannot be in India! Again, there are many causes of corruption, however we may summarize these all causes in a single word and I think you know that word—money! Yes, you correctly think. Money is that honey that everyone wants. Getting and accumulating more and more money is the basic cause of all injustice, fraud and corruptions. And sadly, our all religions, spirituality, and moral and ethical values have been proved failure in stopping people from doing injustice, fraud and corruption.

A study shows that more than 50% of people have first-hand experience of paying bribe or peddling influence to get a job done in a public office. Taxes and bribes are common between state borders; Transparency International estimates that truckers pay annually $5 billion in bribes. Officials often steal government property.

In Bihar, more than 80 per cent of the subsidised food aid to poor is stolen. In cities and villages throughout India, 'mafia raj' consisting of municipal and other government officials, elected politicians, judicial officers, real estate developers and law enforcement officials, acquire, develop and sell land in illegal ways. Many state-funded construction activities in India, such as road and bridge building, are dominated by construction mafia, which are groupings of corrupt public works officials, materials suppliers, politicians and construction contractors. Shoddy construction and material substitution (e.g. mixing sand in cement while submitting expenses for cement) result in roads and highways being dangerous, and sometimes simply washed away when India's heavy monsoon season arrives.

In government hospitals, corruption is associated with non-availability of medicines, getting admission through back-door, consultations with doctors and availing diagnostic services illegally. A study estimates the monetary value of corruption in 11 basic services provided by the government, like education, health-care, judiciary and police to be around Rs.21,068 crores.

Even at religious places, the place where God and goddesses resides, we find corruption. With the power of money and influence, people get direct entry to God and goddesses! Corruptions in religions and at religious places have been beautifully shown in movie 'Oh My God'.

This description of corruption may be continued… and if we start counting scandals, scams, fraud and corruption from India-independence till now; then it is a long list. From 1948 Jeep Scandal—Mr. V. K. Krishna Menon, then India's commissioner in London to 2G and Coal Scams at present, there has been nearly 65 scams and corruption cases happened in India. It means every year a new scam or corruption has been occurred in our country and names of big leaders and politicians have come into light in them. Seeing all these things how can we say—Mera Bharat Mahan!

But, India is great, not because of these few corrupt people, but it is great because of great people like Sri Krishna, Gautama Buddha, Mahavira, Guru Nanak, Vivekananda, Gandhi and many others. I know, due to these scams and corruption, the situation of India is very miserable and critical, but we must think a way-out of this situation. We must make efforts to come out of this situation. We cannot be simply hopeless; only then we can change India.

Leaders and Politicians are Corrupt and We...?: We know very well that our leaders and politicians are selfish, power-seeking and corrupt. We know it because media people repeatedly show us their corrupt activities. I agree that most of leaders and politicians are corrupt—we can lock them in jail as Mr. Amitabh Bachchan locks an answer in KBC! And there is no hope to change them. But the question is what we common men are? Are we milk-washed! Are we honest like Raja Harishchandra! Who is like Raja Harishchandra, I want to meet him and declare him as the tenth wonder of the world!

Reality is that we common people are as cunning and corrupt as our leaders are, but media people do not show our corruption on TV. They do not highlight our cheatings and frauds because showing these little things they will not get a good TRP. They need big issues otherwise awkward things. They cannot show, a dog bites a man, it is a very little issue, it happens in every village and colony. But certainly they can show a man biting a dog; they can show it live to make it more interesting! This is the way media people work.

Reality is that since common men do not get a big and safe opportunity to do a big corruption and therefore, they look honest and uncorrupt, otherwise they are as corrupt as our politicians are. *'Sau me ninyanbe beyeeman, phir bhi mera bhaarat mahan!* Out of 100, 99 are cheaters, still our India is great—is not only for saying but it has some reality.

Ground reality shows that we accept that bribes and cheatings, to some extent, are reasonable and good for our personal-economic-development! We think that without cheating and fraud how one can move ahead of others? Without cheating and fraud, we all would be same—ordinary and common men. Only fraud and corruption make us extra from ordinary and we become extra-ordinary! In addition, reality is that we want to remain fraud and corrupt and continue our corrupt-system as it has been continued from a long back. Mr. Anna Hazare may be interested in eradication of corruption, but we common men are not that much interested. Common men are more interested in hue and cry than good things to come out!

Corruption is deeply rooted in our society. Even rural and villagers are very well acquainted of these terms—*ghoos, chai-paani, baksheesh, nazarana* etc. Once, it so happened that a villager explained me the relation between public, police and crime in a more practical way. He said that if there is no crime occurring at a place, just establish a police station (Thana) there, and then see how crimes are started going up there. I asked him, how? He explained—people have hatred and jealousy from others, from their own relatives and neighbours. For every small and tiny thing they fight like wild animals—like bulls! They kill someone on a tiny issue. And after bull-fighting, they go to police, or police come to them and bribe and corruption started from lower to the higher level. They sell everything even their lands to save themselves from jail and punishment.

I was surprised hearing it but I was agreed as I myself had seen such things happening in my own village and even in my own family. We daily see such news at TV. What does it prove? It proves that we common men are as fraud and corrupt as our leaders and politicians are.

Friends, it does not mean that I want to justify the corruptness of leaders and politicians. No, I just want to say that if we need change, and we want to change India; then we all need to be changed—at least, a little change. Even a little change can make a big difference. I say, be corrupt but in a limit! Don't think that whole money and wealth of the world is yours and it should be only in your bank-account!

In addition, I say if you want to be honest, be honest in your own interest without fearing from police and judiciary system or fearing from religion and God! If I am honest, I am honest in my own interest. Being honest I feel good, happy and peaceful and hence I am honest. I am not honest because I fear from police and judiciary system or religion and God. No, absolutely not. Reality is that I do not fear from anyone. I know I should not speak such things openly but there is no time to hide all these things. It is the need of time to be practical. Again, I know that everyone cannot be like Mahatma Gandhi and Anna Hazare, but I also know that everyone has a soul—a conscience which tells him—to be-good and do-good.

The soul of a person may be weak in power and hence he) may do unsocial and illegal activities, but it does not mean that that person has no soul. No, every person has a soul. No person can be without soul, as no atom and cell can be without a nucleus. So, everyone has a soul and no soul teaches a person to do a bad and an evil thing—I am 100% sure about it. And in fact, I write books only because I know that everyone has a soul—something good which can be made better. I just need to give that soul a power—a power of thinking and sensibility and my work will be done.

Corruption—The Root Cause of Poverty In India: It is a natural law that everything flows from a source of higher concentration to the source of lower concentration. Water, air, heat, energy, electricity and every natural thing follows this nature's law. However, in our human-system, we don't follow this law. In our system, money and wealth flow in a reverse-direction. Here, money flows from poor to the rich—rich are becoming richer and poor are becoming poorer and this cannot be possible without our corrupt mind-set.

Only because of our corrupt mind-set, we do not think about development of one and all. It is a simple thing to understand that if rich will become richer, then how balance and harmony can be maintained in our society. How every person can go above the poverty-line? How India can become a developed country? No, it is not possible.

Therefore, we must understand the situation and help and support one another to maintain balance and harmony in our society. If we do not do this, we will face lots of difficulties like theft, extortion, cheating, fraud, murder etc., and in fact, we are already facing these problems. No one can stop these social evils—even God is helpless in this matter, what to say government, leaders, judiciary system and police-department. No one of them can stop these social evils. So, we must change our mindset and help poor to grow and develop.

We Are All Responsible For Our Problems: As we know, today we are standing among problems – poverty, illiteracy, unemployment, corruption and many others. Now, the question is who is responsible for these problems? Leaders and politicians have their own logics, arguments, policies and planning, and people have their own arguments and crying. We have all some replies and excuses.

We are all blaming each other. Then the question is—who the actual culprit is? Is nature and existence culprit? Are God and goddesses culprit? Is only rich or only poor culprit? Are only politicians and leaders culprits? Are only public servants and bureaucrats culprits? Is only our past generation or only present generation culprit? No, reality is that we are all culprit! We are all responsible for these problems in one way or the other way. Whoever is not making a little effort from his side to eliminate these problems is a culprit. Whoever is involved only in accumulating more and more money is a culprit. Whoever is running the race of power, money and status is a culprit. And, it is ground reality that we are all running this ace. Everyone wants to be first in this race—at least among his surrounding people. At any cost, we want to prove that we are 'above-others', we are superior.

Therefore, we are all culprit and hence responsible for these problems and that's why we are all facing these problems in one way or the other way. Therefore, only blaming others cannot solve our problems. Blaming others is just a tricky way of mind to abstain from our own responsibility, but creator God is observing everyone's trick and it is taking action appropriately. If God converts even a millionaire into a slumdog, so I have nothing more to say in this matter.

Can You Cheat God...Think after Reading This Title?: At present, from top to bottom—at every level, we find fraud and corruption. Honesty and sincerity have been lost from our life. Seeing all these, we think that everyone and everything have been corrupted. However, if we observe this situation from a scientific point of view, then we find that cheating and fraud are only in the human world and not in any other world. If we remove the human-world from the earth, there will no fraud anywhere on this earth. There is no fraud in atomic and molecular world; there is no fraud in nature; there is no fraud in solar system and galaxy. Everywhere there is an integrity and sincerity.

Now, I put this matter in a more practical and simple way: it is true that in the present commercial and corrupt age, we may buy (or influence) anyone in the world, but at the same time, it is also true that we cannot buy a tiny atom of nature. We can cheat or buy a police or a judge—even a policeman of INTERPOL and a judge of international court; but we cannot cheat or buy a tiny atom like Hydrogen. We cannot buy a Hydrogen atom and move it as per our own wish and will. Cheating atoms means we should be expert to eat a bit of KCN (potassium cyanide) without dying! The molecules and atoms of KCN should not react with our inner body-system. Is there anyone on this earth who can cheat atoms in this way? No, there is no one and there can be never anyone.

Therefore, no one can cheat nature and existence and God is nothing but nature and existence. God is made-up of atoms and nothing else. God is not our religious and spiritual old stories and idols, but it is a reality and that reality is in front of us. Open your third-eye, that is, the eye of your sensibility and awareness and see this existence—see from atom to black-hole! These are constituent particles of God. So, come out of this thinking that God is sitting above in sky and He is doing nothing there. He is just sitting idle. No, God is very-very active. We cannot imagine how fast God is acting.

Only a scientist like Newton and Einstein can imagine and try to determine the speed of God and we can read their observation and findings in science. So, God is not just an idol and an imaginary-story but a hard rather the hardest reality. Therefore, understand that we can cheat and buy everyone and everything of man and man-made but we can never cheat and buy even a tiny particle of God. Every God-particle is unsellable—always keep this fact in your mind.

Further, in the present scenario, if we get mental-stress, hypertension, depression, mental-disorder, high BP etc., then we must think that something is going wrong in our life—either our way of living is not healthy or we are doing something wrong. We are doing cheating and fraud and getting reaction of our action—what Newton's third law of motion says. Again, if someone gives logic that now a day everyone is fraud and corrupt, then I must say to him that please change your thinking. You are living with a wrong thinking—expand your observation. Observe total humanity, observe Gautama Buddha to Gandhi, you will find thousands of people who are not fraud and corrupt. Yes, their percentage is less, but it does not mean that on this earth no one is honest and sincere.

So, friends, before doing any cheating and fraud activity, you must think for a while about its future consequences. You must think that you may cheat and buy police and judiciary-system but not tiny atoms and molecules of nature—not the sugar molecules of your body. As your bank account will go up high; your BP and sugar level will also go up high, and one day these sugar molecules will kill you! Therefore, you can never cheat atoms and molecules and hence God.

You must pay for your wrong doings in one way or the other way. You must remind this olden proverb that as you sow so shall you reap! Olden people were not fool and stupid. Their sayings are not absurd. Satyameva Jayate is not just an absurd saying, but a reality and to know this reality you should know and feel science. You should increase your level of sensibility, intelligence and awareness, only then you can experience the truthfulness and sincerity of our olden-and-golden people.

We must be aware that our each and every activity is observed and accounted by God and due to this very observation and accounting, today, someone is a developed and intelligent person like a doctor, engineer, scientist, artist, author etc., whereas most of the people are living at an ordinary level. In addition, due to this very accounting, a person, though taking birth in a poor family develops as a doctor, engineer and a scientist, whereas many people though taking birth in a rich and prosperous family cannot pass even a clerk-grade exam!

Yes it is a truth. You can check the knowledge and efficiency of rich people—especially of leaders and politicians who lead our nation, more that 75% people cannot pass even a clerk-grade exam! This is the reality of India and even of world. So, people like Kabir and Kalam are not lucky and fortunate people, they are not God-gifted people; but they are developed people. They have made sincere effort for their development and they always work in the guidance of their crystallized and strong soul. Otherwise, they are as simple and ordinary as we are. From head to toe, they are exactly like us. They have nothing special except their crystallized and awakened soul, for which they have made sincere efforts.

We Can Ignore Moral and Ethical Values but Not Science: At present, we have mostly discarded goody-goody moral and ethical values of our religions and spirituality. We have discarded olden sayings like 'Honesty is the best policy', 'Truth alone triumphs, 'As you sow so shall you reap' etc. In real life, people follow their own rules and those rules have only one core-value—money, power and status.

Moral and ethical values have become a matter of only teaching and preaching in schools—only in primary schools! Students of high school and college do not read moral and ethical values. They have no time to read such childish subjects and hence education department has removed them from their syllabus. And, primary-school children forget all moral and ethical values when they grow adult. Besides, TV and cinema also make them more practical and hence they leave childish moral stories! With growing, they know our society and India in a better way. They know about cheating, fraud, corruption, rape, murder, extortion, violence in the name of caste, class and religion... everything that is happening in our society. So, we agree that moral and ethical values have been lost from our society.

Don't worry! I also agree that moral and ethical values are only for teaching children at school or at home. They are just goody-goody quotes and ideas and nothing more. They have no power and hence no value, so we can easily ignore them. But, the question is—how can we ignore science and technology and their findings? Because, the findings of science and technology are very real and authentic—they are as real as an electric-shock and we know that an electric-shock is not a good or a bad idea but a real happening, a real process—which can even kill us.

One can ignore or discard a goody-goody quote like 'Honesty is the best policy' or 'As you sow so shall you reap', but how one can discard the Newton's third law of motion, that is—'every action has an equal and opposite reaction'. If one discards this law, he should be an illiterate and ignorant person; otherwise he should be a parrot-type educated person. Sadly, India is full of such educated people. These people are educated only for namesake, and this is a big tragedy of our education system.

Therefore, we should understand that whatever science says about mass and energy and about nature and existence, they are all genuine facts. And we are also a natural body made up of the same mass and energy and the same concept of science works in/on our body. We are not exceptional. We are not divine and special-God-made so that we can be saved by our God even we do bad, unsocial and evil things. No, we are all same—living or non-living, we are all same. We are all made of same atoms.

Hence, before doing any wrong or corrupt thing, we must think for a while about its future reactions and consequences. In fact, we do not know that we could be a zero from a hero and a slum-dog from a millionaire; and therefore we do so many frauds and corruptions. However, it is a reality that millions of past millionaires are present slum-dogs and millions of past slum-dogs are present millionaires and only existence knows their real faces.

Therefore, it is sure that as you sow so shall you reap in one way or the other way. Of course, you may forget your past and present in future; but for the existence, there is no past, present and future. The concept of time is the product of human mind; it is not product of nature and existence. The products of nature and existence are flowers, fragrance, art, music, science, awareness, creativity, evolution, development etc. The existence has been developing from the eternity and it will continue forever.

There is no end of this development. Though, it is sure that one day the sun will lose its total energy and this earth will become a dead planet, it is also sure that the existence will continue developing humanity in some way or the other. Therefore, the findings of science and technology are genuine facts and hence eternal truths. Again, be aware that no guru, god, astrologer, numerologist, or fortuneteller can change these eternal truths. Reality is that most of such people like gurus, gods, astrologers, numerologists etc. are talking non-sense things. They are doing their business to earn money, status and fame by making people fool. So keep distance from these people.

Finally, we should be aware that the creator-existence never punishes anyone—as we think God punishes us for our wrong doings. No, creator-existence never punishes us; instead, it always puts its best effort to develop us, to make us good, kind, honest, creative and intelligent. In fact, it is only we who punish ourselves due to our ego and ignorance. Otherwise, the creator always nurtures and cares us like a mother. Therefore friends, awaken your soul and listen to your inner-voice; there is a call in that voice, a call to move towards peace, honesty, creativity, and development. I can listen to your inner-voice as I can listen to my inner-voice. We have all same inner-voice as we are all children of the same creator-existence.

Only Moral Teachings Are Not Enough to Stop Unsocial Activities: Friends, from the ancient history, we have been learning moral, social and ethical values; however what is its result? The result is in front of us—today all people know and even illiterate people know—what is right and what is wrong, yet most of people are doing illegal and unsocial activities. Lying, cheating and fraud have become a part-(and-parcel!) of our life. Seeing all these, this question naturally raises that despite our long history of moral, social and ethical values, why there is so much cheating and fraud in our society? Why there is difference between our moral-thinking and real-life action? Why we have different teeth for showing and eating!

The answer is very simple—because we have learnt only goody-goody thoughts and ideas from our ancestors and their holy books, but we have not understood and experienced the insight hidden behind their words and hence we are facing problems. Now, the question is, how can we come out of these problems? Answer is only one—self-understanding and self-awakening; because self-awakening is not just a collection of goody-goody words and ideas. It is not just twisting and glamorization of thoughts and ideas, but it is an awakening-state of a soul which observes the truth and reality. It is the developed state of inner-conscience which guides a person to do a right thing and avoid doing a wrong thing. Hence, only self-awakening can transform and develop our society and India. Only this can make us conscious, sensible, virtuous and intelligent, and only this can motivate us to stop unsocial and illegal activities and move on the path of peace, prosperity and development for one and all.

Before Raising Finger Towards Others, Raise Finger Towards Yourself!: There is no doubt that people have more interest in looking bad things than good things. News and media people are doing their business and getting huge amount of money only because of this people's interest and tendency. However, in my life, I have mostly seen and judged my own activities—right or wrong—my inner-conscience has judged them. And hence, at this point, I want to accept my own cheatings and frauds. I accept that during my poverty and unemployment period, due to lack of money, to appear in competitive exams for job I had travel most of my journey by train without-tickets. I wanted to get a job at any cost and after nearly 5 years of struggle I succeeded to get a secured job.

So, a few years back, I was also a poor guy like most of the poor and unemployed youth of India. But, I must say that my soul (inner-consciousness) has never advised me to do cheatings and frauds. While doing any cheating, my soul has asked me—is it a fair to do; cannot you avoid it? I remember, at that time I had argued with my soul in this way: I know it is not fair and good, but I don't know how to tackle this situation; because as you know, my father and also '*mukhiaa*' of my joint-family have refused to give me money for appearing in competitive examinations. In their eyes, I am a failure—as I could not pass either engineering competition or clerk-job competition in 1-2 attempts; and they say that they have no more money to spend (in fact, waste) on me. The *mukhiaa* of my joint-family says, now I should stop my studies and work at home and get married so that my sister could also be married with the help of my dowry-money. What should I do—should I stop appearing in competitive examination; should I live as a poor and unemployed person?... No, I could not live; even you say to live, I could not live. Not only you, even God comes in front of me and says to me to live like a poor, because He has written poverty in my fate and destiny, I could not live. Instead, I will say to God, if you have written poverty in my fate and destiny; then also write next line that

I will become a cheater or a thief! And if you could not write I will write it myself! If you can stop me—try to stop me—but I will do whatever I need to do to eradicate my poverty—right or wrong, I will think later after getting a job. Besides, as you know, I am also earning money rupees 600 a month by taking tuitions of students door-to-door (year 1995-98, staying at Jamshedpur, Bihar, now in Jharkhand). But it is not sufficient for my expenditure. So how can you blame me for my wrong doings? If I am wrong, then my parents and family and even God are wrong, because without any job for me, they have given me birth! They have wasted my time and life. When I had argued with my soul in this way, my soul had no reply, just silence...!

After getting a secured (government) job—where I could live peacefully, when I started thinking about my past activities and experiences, those thinking started taking shape into books—one of which you are studying right now. So, my soul—my consciousness has never advised me to do a wrong thing. It has always asked me to justify my action. It has always advised me to do a good and right thing; and through my writing, if I have written anything good and virtuous, it is only because of my soul.

My soul is my first teacher, guide and director. First, I listen to my soul and then others. My soul does not bear me doing wrong and corrupt things. It scolds me, hates me, reminds me repeatedly my wrong doing and I become irritated, upset and disappointed and I promise to myself that I will not repeat it again—sorry! And with my own experience, I can firmly say that same thing happens with everyone, because everyone has a soul—a conscience and awareness, which always tells a person to do a good thing and avoid doing a bad thing. The self-motivation of a soul may be weak in power but everyone has a soul, it is 100% sure; and through my writings, I want to stimulate the same awakening power of soul, so that people naturally do good things and avoid doing bad things.

You know why I am writing continuously even though I am not a famous writer and I have been proved a failure in writing—as my three books did not do well, people have no interest in my books. From last 9 years (after my first book released in 2004), my wife has been continuously advising me to stop writing. She usually says, you are wasting your time—nothing is going to change. People and society will always remain like this—cheating, fraud, corruption, rape, murder, violence will always continue. Your book can do nothing. There are many books, and better books than yours, but what is happening—nothing. We have Gita, Ramayana, Koran, Bible, and many others—but what is happening—nothing! No one cares these books! People read these books only for namesake, just to do religious-formalities.

They do not follow the ideas and messages of these books. Also, it is India and here everything is slow and change will also come sl ›wly. Besides, you are also not a mahatma, you have also done cheating during your struggling period; then why are you becoming a social-reformer now! Let others do what they are doing; who are you to change them? And why are you interested to change them, what is your selfishness and benefit? Leave benefit—you have lost my twenty five thousand rupees only because of your writing and with bank-interest it should be doubled now. So, you are a looser in every way. (To publish my first book—Khud Phaisala Karo Dost, I had spend twenty five thousand rupees, and sadly, this money was my wife's! So, you can understand my position.) And this thinking and mentality is not only of my wife but most of the people of India and world; and this is the basic reason that India is not changing. We need to change this thinking and mentality that India can never change, only then we can change India.

Even I am failure in writing; I continued my writing because my soul motivates me to continue it. My soul says—you continue your effort, you can bring out a little change in people and society. And, do not think that you are a failure; instead, you think that you are reaching your boiling point! You are giving more heat and light in your writing. So, continue your effort, one day people will listen to you; and I do not know people will listen to me or not but I cannot stop making efforts. So, our soul is great. It is always great because our creator is great. Only our mind—our thinking and way of looking to our people and society has been corrupted. It needs change and it must be changed, only then we can change our society and country.

Existence Has Its Own Mechanism to Move Forward: Fraud and corruption have such a large impact on our society that, it seems there is no hope to change our society and country. Police and law are working only for namesake; people have not faith and trust in them. Rich are becoming richer and poor are becoming poorer. It appears that there is no fair and unbiased mechanism working in this existence.

However, we should not be hopeless and disappointed, and for that, we need to see this whole matter with a broad prospective. We need to see the positive and bright-side of humanity. We need to see the development of science and humanity. Is it not a fact that we have made a tremendous progress in science and technology? Is it not a fact that we have developed from primitive Stone Age to the modern science age? Yes, it is a fact. We have invented many devices to make our life easy and comfortable. In fact, due to these very comfortable devices, today people do not dream to go to heaven; instead, they want to enjoy luxury of heaven on this very earth! So, how do we achieve this great development? We achieve this because the actual controller and organizer of the humanity is our creator-existence and not our police and law, leaders and politicians, and gurus and gods. This existence does not function as per man-made policies and principles; instead it functions as per its own awareness and intelligence and about its functional-mechanism, only science makes a genuine effort to know and experience. Only science is most-close to the truth of nature and existence. Hence, we may consider all man-made policies and principles, and laws and orders as fake and phony; but we cannot ignore the findings of science and technology. Therefore, understand that because existence controls and guides all activities of humanity, we have developed to this modern level.

Now, it is up to you, in what direction you want to move. You want to move in the direction of science, art, creativity, development; or you want to move in the direction of cheating, fraud, corruption, money and power. But one thing is sure that one day you must move in the direction of science, creativity and development, because the future of humanity is of science, creativity and total-development. If you will not move in that direction, you will be lagged behind and existence will drag you by force to move you in that direction. This existence cannot leave you stand behind. It cannot leave anyone as it has responsibility to develop everyone. In fact, existence is already dragging many people to move in that direction. If you are one of them, leave your rigidness and start moving in that direction. Help existence to move you.

3 Critical Issues That Plague Us

We Need a Change In Our Election System

If we want to change and develop India, we urgently need a big change in our election system. First of all, we need to abolish many political parties system. No Congress, BJP, Left-Right-Centre, Third and Fourth Front—nothing, all political parties should be abolished. Sensible, capable and intelligent people will represent and lead our states and country and not a party. Even our beloved leader Mahatma Gandhi wanted that Congress party should be abolished after getting independence of India; since in his very own life-time, he had seen the selfishness and power-seeking nature of political people in his own party. However, here, I don't want to say that leaders of only Congress Party are selfish and power-seeking; no, not at all. I consider that every party has sensible and intelligent people, and reversely, every party has selfish and power-seeking people. So, I don't want to raise finger towards only a single party.

Friends, if even after 66 years of independence of India, our nation is in such a poor and downtrodden condition, its 50% people are still in a poor and miserable position; then we must need a change in our election system, because it shows that we are not selecting sensible, capable and intelligent leaders who can develop our country. Otherwise, it shows that India has not power to produce sensible, capable and intelligent leaders!? I think, and I consider that all the people of India will be agreed with me on this point that a land of Buddha and Sri Krishna, and Subas, Sardar Patel and Gandhi cannot have scarcity of sensible and intelligent leaders. So the matter is only this that we are not just selecting the correct leaders and it shows shortcomings and drawbacks of our election system.

Therefore, with due respect and regards, I request all the intelligent and sincere people and leaders of India, like MLAs, MPs, CMs, PM, Presidents of all political parties, Election Commissioner, Chief Justice of India, and President of India, that we, the common men and especially youths of India, need a change in our election system. Of course, India has democracy and it is the finest system to maintain equality, peace and harmony in our society; but we need to utilize this concept in a proper manner.

For this, first we need that our election-system should be more fair, sensible, common, less-expensive and general—as it is also called general-election; so that it can be under reach to every citizen of India. Second important change we need is that—as for a job, a common man appears in a competitive examination—written, interview, group-discussion, mental, psychological, physical and medical tests, and then police verification for our character-verification; and after these many tests we get an opportunity to serve our nation or a state or a company. Likewise, before becoming an MLA or MP, a person should go through a similar kind of test—in fact an IAS and CDS level test. Then, the top candidates will be selected for public-voting and among them, the top candidates will be selected for the posts of MLA, MP, CM, PM and President of India. In fact, for these posts, the competition should be the toughest one.

At present, Supreme Court has given directives that in the coming election in 2014, we shall get a new option in the voting machine, that is—NOTA, means none of the above.

But, the question is, can it solve our problem, because if most of people reject all the candidates, then what will happen? In that case, I think, there should be an option like—president rule, but it is not so.

Anyway, the first and foremost change we need is that every candidate should go under a filter test—a CDS or IAS level test. Of course, since this will be a filter-test for leaders, so more weightage will be given to test leadership quality of the candidates like their decision-making power, mental and reasoning ability, IQ-test, speech delivery to influence people etc. If we do this single change in election system, many sensible, capable and intelligent people will come and join in parliament-house and state-assemblies and lead this country on the path of prosperity and development.

I myself want to go through this test for the post of education-minster (I am not making joke); either for a state, especially for Bihar (I am from Bihar and the position of Bihar in literacy is not good, but it is improving slowly) or for central government. After becoming education-minister, my first aim will be educating every child of India. I will teach and motivate them in my own way as I feel that I have a little potential to be a teacher. I know I am not a very efficient candidate. I have been proved failure at many places, but I must make effort and attempt.

Today, if I am a little successful person, it is only because I have made many attempts. My view towards life is very simple—I am here on this earth to make effort and attempt. So, I do my best and leave the rest of things to God, and I want to give the same message to everyone. Hence, eat nutritious and delicious food and make effort life-long! Life has no death; so if you are very interested to make efforts and attempts, you may come back again here to make efforts. I am in the middle—neither more nor less, and since I am doing my best in this very life, so I will not come back again here soon. In fact, I want to come back on this earth when there will be no poverty on this earth and that's why I want to change India and this world—where every person will be employed and above poverty line.

However, my aim is very big and hence, I need help and support of everyone. Without help and support of everyone, my aim can never be achieved by me or by anyone—even God is included in this anyone-list! God can do nothing without our help and support. We are the fingers of God, so without our help and support God can do nothing.

However, in the present scenario, for a common man, going to the post of education minister, is a very difficult task. If I go directly to a political party or a leader, no party or leader will entertain me. I have gone to some leaders, not to join their party but just to present my book for their compliments, but at many occasions, I have been not allowed to meet them directly. Secondly, in election, if I stand as an individual candidate, no one will vote me—even my wife is against me! She just wants me to do government job and move to-and-fro between home and office—don't do anything else. Let happen whatever is happening in India and world, no one can change them. Whatever I want to do for people and nation (or a little bit for world), I do it because of my inner-inspiration, my soul. So, you can understand my position and I think, same is the situation of most of the common men who want to do something sincerely for India.

Friends, if we choose even a clerk-grade employee after taking many tests, then we must be very-very careful before selecting a leader for our area, state and nation. We cannot simply handover our area, state and country in the hands of anyone, who may be an illiterate, inefficient and fraud, and has been elected because of his power, influence and money. Even political parties are not demolished, because no party will be agreed for this, every candidate must go through a CDS or IAS level test and I think this is the responsibility of election commission and judiciary system—especially of Supreme Court of India. And I am such a man who, if such a filter test is not implemented, cannot cast his valuable vote. I am not blind and I cannot select anyone blindly to lead my area, state and country. Let other people cast their votes as per their choices and preferences—caste, class, race, region, religion, donation etc., but I cannot cast my vote.

In the present scenario, as poet Tulsidas says—*koi nrip hoye hame kya haani*, let anyone be a king or a minister, we have no loss (or gain either), and therefore, I ignore casting my vote. I can cast my vote only to eligible candidates, who will go through a CDS or IAS-level filter test. Yes, I know even a CDS or IAS pass candidate may be a corrupt one, but I am sure that the wisdom, conscience and sensibility level of such a candidate will be many times better and higher than that of most of our present politicians and leaders, and hence I can trust his wisdom, conscience and sensibility.

Finally, I know there are many ifs and buts and shoulds and shouldn'ts in—what I have said above, but I am sure if we follow the above filter-test, we must get a good change in our system and in India. I hope, and I am sure that top-level, sincere and intelligent people of India will notice and care my points, and for this, I and whole nation will be ever grateful to them.

A Letter to the Media People

Dear Media People/Friends,

As you know, press and media have a great responsibility in building a good society and nation and a good world as well. You are a great source of information, education and entertainment. You have a great role in informing and awakening people and society for a rapid social change. You have power to speak boldly against frauds, corruption and every evil thing which are damaging our society and nation. That's why you are considered as the fourth pillar of our nation. Therefore, I request you to find out more and more new and creative ways to awaken and develop our people, society and nation. Spread knowledge and awareness in public and society. Minimize bad news and give more places to good news. Only bad things are not happening in our society and nation. So, also see good news and give more places to good news so that people can see the goodness of people and society and be motivated to do something good for others.

Today, most of the news channels preferably show bad and sensitive news. Here is a sample of Non-Stop-100 news of top news channels: 10 murders; 10 rapes and sexual harassments; 10 cheatings, fraud, theft and extortions; 10 scams and corruptions; 10-15 political news—politics, diplomacy and blame-game of political leaders; 5-10 road accidents; 5-10 world events—mostly about politics and calamities; 5-10 sports news; 5-8 miscellaneous news; and 2-3 good news in exception! Every day you people collect similar stories and news and show us full day. You show us news as if nothing is happening good and virtuous in our society, nation and in the world.

Think for a while... daily, nearly 80 crores people in India and nearly 4 billion people in world work somewhere (office, factory, school etc.) and return to their home safely—is it not good news? Daily, nearly 20 crores of children and young Indians go to their schools and colleges and learn something there and return to their home safely—is it not good news? Daily, at least 90% state and central government employees work sincerely for growth and development of India—is it not good news (you may consider 10% as dishonest and corrupt, but I am not interested in these people and highlight them)? Daily, at least 60-70% leaders think and make plan and start implementing their plan honestly (or with 5-10% corruption!)— is it not good news?

This list may go long…..but in short, I want to say that there are many times more good things are happening in our society than bad things. You just need a good intention to see all these good things and making them news. If you see only TRP of your news-channel and your salary-package then you will see and collect only such bad news.

Remember, if you think that just by showing bad news, you can inform and awaken people and change our society and nation; then you are on a wrong thinking. To change people and society, it needs a lot of thinking, self-awareness, study, analysis, practical-observation, creativity, efforts, experiments and many things more… and even then, it is not sure that we will succeed to change our society and nation or not. So, it is not an easy task.

There is a long-list of great-failures in this filed—from Gautama Buddha to Gandhi, there are many great failures! Of course, we consider them great people (I too), but ground reality shows that their aim is not fulfilled yet. Still most of the people are in poor and miserable condition, so such great people are great failures!

Therefore, before showing any news, think deeply about its impact on our society and nation—and especially on our children and young-India, because they are very soft, sensitive and vulnerable. So, considering the children and youth of India as the future of India, you must be selective, sensitive and reflective while showing news. I hope you sensitive, intelligent and responsible people will care my words to change India.

With warm regards,
Abhay,
A Common-man

Criminalism, Naxalism and Terrorism: I want to say government and all the leaders of India and world that, first of all, we need to eradicate poverty, unemployment and illiteracy from all over the world and then we should think about eradicating problems of naxalism and terrorism. If a person becomes a thief, naxalite or a terrorist because of his poverty and unemployment then I have sympathy with him. In fact, I myself had decided in my teenage that poverty may make me anything except a beggar. (My joint-family had usually warned that if they would separate me from the joint-family, I would become a beggar. So I had a deep abhorrence towards begging. Perhaps, due to this deep abhorrence, I could not be a beggar even in my next birth!) And see, a person, who can think and make effort for development of India and total humanity; how poverty and unemployment spoil his thinking and action.

Therefore, first we need to make effort to eradicate poverty and unemployment, and then we have to think about eradication of naxalism and terrorism. Just making stringent laws and orders and strict punishments, we cannot solve these problems. Our grandfathers and fathers have given birth to enough children, so we can hang everyday 15-20 thieves, criminals and terrorists! There are lakhs and crores of thieves, criminals and terrorists, so we can do this cruel-exercise everyday!

Have you ever thought, one day you may be also one of these thieves and criminals. You may have to do illegal and unsocial things to eradicate your poverty. I have often thought about it; because, as you know, I am also a little-corrupt person! I am not a saint or mahatma. As a matter of fact, since I am a little corrupt one, I am here doing a job and earning enough salary to enjoy a happy life. Otherwise, I would have been living like my father—living a miser, dull and dead life—counting and saving every single coin. Even in his rupees 2000 monthly income, he wanted to save rupees 500! Such a miser person he is.

And because I am a little corrupt one, for me, it is a difficult thing to kill someone—to hang someone. No, I may keep someone in jail for his whole life—let him die in jail, but I can never kill someone in a moment of time. In my awareness, it is inhuman to kill someone. As a matter of fact, if I am a vegetarian in nature, it is only because I do not like killing anything (of course, being a vegetarian, I kill plants, vegetables and fruits, but there is no other way to live). I feel pain and uneasiness when I see someone killing an animal—even a fish.

So, before hanging and killing someone—even a thief or a criminal, we must be very careful and awaken: we must think ten times—is it right…? Can I avoid it? Can I do something better for that thief and criminal—which can change his life? Why someone turns into a thief or a criminal? Have I time and patience to know every minutes of his life? There are many such questions on which we should ponder over deeply before taking any final decision.

If we look at daily news, we can realize that youth is losing touch with our society and nation. They are losing their conscience and sensibility—the sense of right and wrong. Due to increasing unemployment, they are doing cheating, fraud, loot and even murder. This is happening because we have failed to channelize their energy in a right direction. We have been failed to help them in realizing their inner-virtue, imaginations and creativity. We have failed to give them appropriate opportunities—leave right kind of opportunity; we are not able to give them even a labour, peon and clerk grade job.

But parents, family, leaders and government do not see their own mistakes. They simply see mistakes of only youths. No, this is not fair and justice. Ground reality is that our forefathers and parents have done mistakes due to their ignorance, and now, we—the youths of India have to correct those mistakes. There is no way except correcting our forefather's mistake. We have to control population. We have to eradicate illiteracy and false myths and beliefs. We may have to live one whole life as an unemployed and hence poor. I know it is very difficult to bear the pain of poverty and unemployment, because only in 5 years, I was nearly died. I was living but I had started dying! My patience and courage were dying. So, I can better understand and experience the pain and difficulties of my youth friends.

Look at our youth overseas, they are working wonders. We are surprised seeing their achievements. Why can't these young people do the same job here in this country? Why are we facing brain-drain? The answer lies in the lack of opportunities which they find in plenty in other countries. The loss is completely ours. And please stop talking and singing songs of patriotism now and then. Young-generation is very practical and sensible. They need opportunities to show their talents and creativity.

It is the story of olden days that political leaders will deliver emotional speech about patriotism, peace and harmony, and youth will simply listen to their speech—it cannot go anymore. Political leaders will enjoy a luxury life and youth and public will suffer—it cannot go anymore. Common men are not here only to hear your speech; instead we are here to work, to show our talents and creativity, and in returns we want a good salary to enjoy a happy life. Therefore, leaders and politicians; please understand and awake and do something for people and youth. It is high time to prevent our youth from going in wrong directions by providing them better opportunities and employment. Make such policies which aim at empowering our youth so that we can be assured of a better future of our India.

Friends, if we want to change India, we must all think and act for it. If we want to come out of root-level problems like poverty, unemployment and other social evils, we must all need to think a way-out. I am also one of you thinking a way-out. I am not a writer and writing is not my profession and never can it be. So friends, by doing cheating, fraud, loot and murder etc.—we may be safe for a few days, months or years, but in the long run of our life, we must face these problems again and again.

Additionally, I know that it is very easy to talk about social problems and difficulties than tackling and solving them. However, looking to our future, we must develop our patience and sensibility and we should take correct steps to tackle these problems. Otherwise our miserable and poor India will become even more miserable and poor. Now, it is in our hand to make it more miserable and poor or shape and move it on the path of development and prosperity.

If you really love India and love those people who have sacrificed their life for our freedom and development, I think, even you are on the wrong path; you will come back and join your hands to build a developed India. We need all to join our hands and work together to make a clean, healthy and prosperous India.

War and Peace with Pakistan/China: President of America Mr. Jorge Washington has once said, 'If you want peace, be ready for war.' Is it really true? Because, I do not see any relation between war and peace except that they are diametrically-opposite. Why should we be ready for war if we want peace? Someone may argue that our enemy may invade and capture us, and this has been already happened with many countries including India.

Ok, then, in the present nuclear-power age, a few atom and hydrogen bombs are enough to fight and destroy any country of the world. So, every country should prepare 20 hydrogen bombs and be ready for war. In case of war, we will play a 20-20 cricket match with bombs and within a few hours the result of the match will be declared. Even without the actual match, I can declare the result, the result will be—total destruction; destruction of humanity, destruction of this beautiful earth.

Moreover, fighting small wars and killing 5, 10 or 50 soldiers now and then—as it happens between India and Pakistan, is totally childish. War means—kill or be killed, just finish the game forever; and every country must think in this way. In my view, make war policy of only one sentence—I will not begin fight or war with any country, but in counterattack, if I start fighting, I will start with hydrogen bombs, that's all. If I would become defense minister of any country (in fact, I think about total humanity and not about just India.); my war policy will of only this one sentence. In policy, I don't like so many ifs and buts, terms and conditions, rules and regulations, fight-of-tongues and cold-war. No, these are all useless things in modern age. Modern age means—we should be logical, sensible, scientific and quick in our decision and action.

In this connection, here I would like to share an incident which had been occurred with me during a train journey.

It is one of bitter experiences of my life when a discussion turned into an argument and then it became violent. Once, I was traveling by train in an army bogy. Army people were busy in talking about different issues like cinema, cricket, politics—usual gossip. I was hearing their discussion without any involvement.

While discussing politics, at a certain point, one person told, 'President is the king of our country.' (*President desh ka raja hota hai.*) Hearing his words, I could not stop myself involving in their discussion. I said in an enquiring manner, 'In past ages, there were used to be kings and queens in our country. At present, there is no one king or queen in our country. President of India is the supreme commander of our country with some other responsibilities and administrative powers. But it does not mean that he is the king of our country'. That army person argued me, 'Any time our president may give order to attack on Pakistan and only a king can do this.' I said, 'No, president cannot give such an order without a serious issue. But I can see, a person like you can easily give such an order. And, Pakistan is not as weak as you consider, if you can destroy him, he can also destroy us to the maximum level.'

Hearing my words, most of the people were started asking me whether I am a Pakistani, and if not, why I am supporting Pakistan? I replied, 'First, I am a human being. I am also an Indian like you. I am just saying the reality.' But all people were opposing me and supporting the army personnel. All people were putting pressure on me to keep quit. But, I could not keep quit and it proved a big mistake for me. And as soon as I opened my mouth to speak further, the army personnel gave a hard punch on my face! I was surprised, awkward and feeling nervous and embarrassed. I had never expected this. My mouth started bleeding. Besides, he warned me, 'If you would say just a single word more, I will throw you out of the train.' He might have abused me, too; but I could not dare to speak a single word further.

After getting his huge punch and abusive words, I had thought within, 'What is the use of arguing these people? Let them think whatever they think. Let them think anyone as their king or queen, or god or goddess. It is not easy to make them understand the reality. So, you better keep quite.' And I had stopped talking to those people; there was no use of it. However, latter I had observed that slowly those people had started paying attention on my words and they had agreed that there is a reality and practicality in my words.

Friends, our first and foremost view must be—war is always cruel and destructive. It always brings damages, destruction, pain, misery and sorrow. It is rarely fruitful. Peace is the first-way and war is the last-way. War is not a way but it is a dead-end. It is destruction and destruction can never be called a way. Creation and creativity is a way. War shows our ego, ignorance and wildness. It shows that still we are wild-animals. We may be living in modern science age, but still we are animals.

We have seen first and second world-wars and we know their results very well. They have been proved many times more destructive, damaging and painful than any use. Therefore, we must avoid all types of war—even a little war is dangerous. All countries must think with a friendly and developing approach for development of a healthy and balanced humanity. We should help and support each other for solving our problems. Especially India and Pakistan are facing lots of root-level problems like poverty and unemployment and they must think with a friendly approach to solve them. Peace is the first and basic requirement of development.

And, here, in a polite manner, I want to say that I am not agreed with Mr. Jorge Washington's saying that, for peace, we need to be ready for war. No, for being peaceful, we just need to be peaceful. We just need basic needs of our life like food, cloth and shelter. We need a healthy thinking and we need a little fun, music and entertainment! So, it is illogical, unholy and wrong thinking that for being peaceful, we need to be ready for war. Therefore, we must avoid all types of violence and wars. We should destroy our dangerous nuclear weapons with a mutual understanding and agreement, and we should help each other for developing a healthy and balanced humanity.

Finally, we must be aware that we can never destroy 'life' from the earth. In case of war, existence will again start sprouting 'life' from that point of destruction, where we will leave it due to our stupidity and ego. Einstein had rightly remarked when he had been asked about third world war. He had told that he could not tell about third world war, but he could tell about forth world war. We will fight forth world war with stones and axes! What an intelligent imagination! Really dear Einstein is an expert in both scientific as well as practical imagination. Therefore, if we consider that we are the highest developed and intelligent creation of the existence, we should help existence in its better evolution and development. Creativity and creation should be our aim and not war and destruction. ✌

4

Friends! Be Bold and Self-Reliant

Be Bold and Self-Reliant

This chapter is especially for girls and women. First of all, I want to say them that whatever may be the cause of difficulty and problem in your life—dowry, divorce, domestic-violence, rape, sexual harassments or any cause, the first thing you need to solve your problem is—try to become self-dependent, especially in monetary sense. If a woman is self-employed and she earns good enough to live independently, her husband and family cannot harass her. Because, she can easily take decision to live independently; and certainly every woman who is facing such problems should take this decision. Break family barrier and live alone—this is the only way to live with self-respect and dignity. If required, do hard-work and struggle for a better survival. Do not depend on anyone, even on your parents. Never think to live like a parasite. In India, most of the women are living as parasites depending on their husbands and families and this is the basic cause of their pain and misery. Women and especially young-women must change this parasitic-attitude. They must try to be strong and self-reliant. Without your strength and cooperation, India cannot change and become a developed country.

To stop violence against woman, the first thing Indian-leaders and government should do is that they should give employment to every woman who needs a job. This single step can stop most of domestic-violence and discriminations against women. My mother has faced many such problems only because she was unemployed and hence poor. Even my father was unemployed, what to say about my mother. In India, most of the women are unemployed, so my mother is not an exception. My mother was dependent on her family for everything. In fact, I have no words to describe my mother's all difficulties and sufferings. I can only feel her sufferings and sometimes shed tears. But only shedding tears and screaming are not going to solve our problems. We have to work and make efforts to be self-dependent—this is the only way.

After my marriage, I had said many times to my wife (a graduate) that even you don't want to do a permanent job; at least, you should check your potential and ability. You should do what you want to do. You should fulfill your all desires and this is the right time to fulfill your desires. With age, our desires start slowly dying. In addition, it is possible that at some point of time in your life, you may have to work and earn money. So if you make practice now, you can easily handle that situation. You just be sure that you can earn money and survive on your own ability. With this motivation, she started teaching in a private school and she also completed a teacher training course. But the problem is, due to huge population and huge number of unemployed educated youth, just to earn 3 to 5 thousand rupees a month; we have to work hard in a private institution/company, and still we do not get any respect and dignity from our employer. So, my wife left her job and now she is purely a house wife.

Seeing difficulties of women, I must say all girl-friends of India and world (I hope, you won't mind me saying you girl-friends! However, in real life, I have only one girl-friend and that is my wife.) that first be bold and then beautiful. Boldness and self-reliance are more important than beautifulness.

Of course, man-world is crazy for your beautiful body, but men are crazy to use-and-throw you and not love you—always mind it. So, it is more important to give knowledge and power to your brain and body than cream and cosmetics to your body. I am saying this because today cream and cosmetics market is very hot. So, before beautifying your body give power and energy to your brain and soul—the power of knowledge, self-confidence and self-reliance; and most importantly the power of money!

Rape and Sexual-Harassment: Simply making strong and stringent laws and rules and regulations are not going to solve this problem. Surely, it will bring a little change in thinking of wild-nature people, but to eradicate this problem completely, we all have to make effort. Especially, parents, teachers, TV, cinema and media should take responsibility to give our children and youths a good and healthy thinking and attitude towards girls and women. Sexual-materials, rape and violent scenes shown in the films and TV are severely damaging the thinking and attitude of children and teenagers. However, TV and cinema-industry have their own excuses. They argue that they show us these things because such things and incidences happen in our society. They argue that they just reflect our society acting as a mirror. But my question and also request to TV, cinema and media people is that only bad and violent things are not happening in our society. Good and virtuous things are also happening; so make a proper balance in both, so that people may see the real picture of our society.

Further, we demand for a strong law like—Kill or hang the rapist. But the question is who is going to implement these strong laws on ground—policeman, lawyer and judge. But these people can be influenced by money; they can be heavily bribed? Most of corrupts and rapists are safe only because of this very reason. We can blame policemen and laws for this, but just blaming cannot give us solution. Besides, police and law argue that they cannot take care of everyone acting as a 'bodyguard' for everyone. Leaders and government promise us many times that for them, safety and security of common men is their first priority, but we know about their commitment and sincerity. So, we cannot simply depend on their false promises.

Hence, the only solution comes out is that we must take care of ourselves. Every parents and family should care of their children—where their children are going and what they are doing there, a parent should know about it. And most importantly, one thing we must remember that to take care of us, even our parents cannot be always with us. So, every individual must take care of himself/herself. We have to be always alert and awake for our safety and security, and if required to face such kind of challenges.

While facing such kind of challenges, please note that always fighting is not the way, sometimes we may have to flight as modern psychologists suggest—'fight or flight!' We just need to try to come out of that 'fatal' situation and later, we may counter attack taking help of police, if required. So, there is no readymade way and hard-and-fast rules to tackle such situations. We can only cleverly tackle such situations using our presence of mind. Also, we cannot simply hope and pray God that our surrounding people may become good, helpful and kind. No, it cannot happen just by praying God. Surely, God is making effort for it, but we also need to make effort for it. God is helpless without our support.

Dowry and Domestic Violence: In place of making laws and orders to stop dowry-system and domestic-violence, I have a simple request to the leaders and government of India that, you provide employment to every woman. Kindly make them financially-self-dependent. No woman should remain dependent on her parents, husband or family. In that situation, a husband or a family cannot harass a woman, because that woman will come out of that family and start living alone. She can show her thumb to her husband and family and I want every woman should be bold enough to do that.

But, leaders and politicians cannot do this. They will give only ideas and make and amend rules and regulations. Ok, let them do their duties and formalities and people do their own, and let continue dowry and domestic-violence as usual! Understand that, in a relation, if there is mutual-understanding and friendliness, no rules and regulations are required, but if there is no mutual-understanding and friendliness then not only constitutional laws but also Newton's third law is required, that is—tit for tat! I am also a man of tit for tat! I am such a man who maintains this relation even with God! I do not consider myself as a slave or servant of God but a friend of God, and I say, you also maintain the same relation with everyone and even with God. Live with self-respect and dignity and not as a slave.

Now, I would like to ask parents—why do you want to marry your daughter free of cost? Why do you want to make your daughter a beggar or a servant of others? Why do you want kindness and sympathy from others? I have seen dowry-less marriage in my own family. One of my grandfathers, who was richest in my joint family, had married three times!—once with dowry and twice dowry-free! Why? To get children—he had not got any child from his first wife and hence he had married thrice at the age of 50. So, only childless old-men or widowers can do such marriages and you know the reason behind these marriages.

Therefore, please stop expecting anything without something in our society. In this commercial and professional age, nothing is free. See! My rich-grandfather had married twice dowry-free for children but once when I had asked 1000 rupees for my studies—he had no money for me. He can spend lakhs of rupees for his own children (now, he had got three children from his third wife), but he had no money for a boy who belongs to his own family. You know, he had spent nearly two lakhs rupees (year 1984-87) to build a temple of Lord Siva for getting a child, but he had never thought to spend a few thousand rupees on my studies. This is the reality of a joint-family of India, which is famous for its family-values all over the world.

Therefore, nothing is free in our family and society. So, be prepared to buy a thing that you want, or be freely available—rich people will take you their homes and use you—and hope they will not throw you! Otherwise, stand like a beggar along roadside or a temple, people of India are still humble for beggars. They can give you enough to feed your stomach. Sorry friends, I have no goody-goody speech. See religious and spiritual TV channel shows like Aastha and Sanskar; there you will find lots of goody-goody speeches. Perhaps, they will better counsel you and give you Peace-of-Mind. My soul and my God tell me to speak-out reality and not goody-goody speeches. So you can expect only reality from me. Be aware that only accepting reality and making effort with understanding can solve our problems and not goody-goody speeches or positive thinking.

Further, this is the constitutional law that all children of a couple have equal right to share their parents' property. So, a parent should give the shared amount to her daughter at the time of her marriage and finish this financial-crisis! According to the value of that amount, search a boy for your daughter to marry her; otherwise give this amount to her and let her free to decide herself to marry or not. As we know, our society is a market place, and we have to search and select a bridegroom to marry our daughter or sister (I have a sister, and here I am sharing my own experiences). Therefore, while selecting a bridegroom, fix a price for everything as we do in a business-deal and then be honest.

Now, if we are honest, how harassment and domestic-violence due to dowry can happen in a family? No, it can never happen. Domestic-violence starts only when we become dishonest and greedy. And, in a dishonest and greedy relation, there is only one way or solution—break family barrier, take divorce, be self-dependent, live alone or as you like; you can also marry again. This is the only way to live with self-respect and dignity. (I have no experience about divorce and second marriage, so I cannot say anything about it.)

Moreover, as usual, we generally think that in all cases, bridegroom family members are guilty for dowry-crimes. However, sometimes the real matter happens to be a different one. Many times, it happens that bride-side promises to give a huge amount in dowry, but their basic intension is to cheat the bridegroom's parent. Initially, they give some amount to catch the fish in the net, and after that, they show their real faces. Even they blackmail bridegroom's parents saying that they will go to police and law. This is also a face of our fraud society. Seeing all these cheating and fraud—I also feel to say—*sau me ninyanbe beyeeman, phir bhi mera bhaarat mahan!* (Out of 100, 99 are cheaters, yet our India is great!)

No doubt, harassment and domestic-violence for dowry is bad, but think for a while: violence is due to dowry or violence is due to our greed for money. Dowry (money) is a problem or our greed is a problem? And you know the answer. We want simple and easy way to earn money and taking more and more dowry is one of the simplest ways of it. Now, what is the solution of our greed? How can we leave our greed? We have been hearing gurus and mahatmas from thousands of years and all gurus and mahatmas have said—greed is bad, leave greed. But greed is not leaving us. And therefore, I think, modern-sensible people have accepted that—greed is good! We do not need to leave greed! We can live with greed.

Then what is the way—only one, provide employment to every woman—make them financially-self-dependent. Let them free to live independently. They have better conscience and sensibility than men, so they can think better about their way of living. Otherwise, a girl or woman should make effort herself to be self-reliant. Yes, you may need to struggle, you struggle; there is no other way. Struggle for your better survival or you will die!

What Is Fair In Love?: It is said that everything is fair in love and war; however I am not agreed with this quote. In war, everything may be fair; but in love everything can never be fair. In war, we can do anything; we can destroy even the whole world, but it is not easy to give even a slap to our lover. However, in real life, people are not only slapping their lovers but also they are killing them. What a love! If this is love, then what is hatred!

There are many causes of hatred and violence in love, but reality is that the cause of any hatred and violence is lack of understanding and awareness and nothing else. Reality is that in love, there is not a little place for quarrel and violence. Violence is like antonym of love; so violence can take place at any place except in love. In this matter, I try to go in a practical manner: suppose you (male) happen to be in love with someone and after a few months or years, your lover refused to share her love with you. She refused to spend her life with you. As per my experience, love is nothing but friendliness between two persons; it is sharing of our thinking, feelings, emotions, and at the end—our souls, our beings.

So, in love, we share everything with our lover. But, in case, due to any cause, or even without any cause—just a mood-swing or flirt (*meri marji!*), if our lover refuses to share her love with us, it does not mean that we would be angered and punish her. Why and how can we punish her, who are we to punish her? No, it is only our stupidity and wildness to capture and punish someone. It shows that we are still animal. Otherwise, God has created all of us to live free and independent. God wants only a friendly relation among us and no any other relation. So, no one should force other to live under him like a slave.

You know, I had asked my lover and now my wife, Priyanka, three times—do you want to marry me—just to confirm that she really wants to marry me! I had an arranged marriage but even in an arranged marriage I had fallen (not fallen but raised!) in love with her. First time, I had met her in a relative's house without any pre-plan. At village, I had come out of my home with an aim to search a suitable bridegroom for my sister and in the way, I found a girl, fell in love with her, and finally I made her my bride. So, my love-story is a true *chalate-chalate* type story. Priyanka had come to her relative's home (in a village) with her mother for *chhath-puja* (a worship of sun). Her parents were also planning to marry her and I was also a considerable candidate in their mind. So, in our first meeting, for the first time, after a brief conversation or say inter-view with her, in front of all family members, I had asked her—do you want to marry me, or is there any problem with you? Within 5 minutes conversation with her, I had come to the main point directly! (I am this type of man. Come to the main point as quickly as possible—make story as little as possible.) She had replied me instantly, "No…, I have no problem." Even she had repeated her words, "No… no…" Hearing her instant reply, something shocked within me. I asked her, "Do you want to ask me anything about me, (as till now, she had not asked me anything. She started asking me only after marriage!)" She replied, "No, I have nothing to ask." Although, she is a graduate from political science, yet she did not ask me anything. Most importantly, she did not take even a second to think, decide and choose a person, to whom she is going to marry; she is going to live her whole life! What a surprise! Really, I was surprised. I was thinking within—such a deep trust on an unknown person! What a girl! It seems that if I say, Ok, then, let's marry me now and she is ready! And because of her deep trust or say blind-trust on me, I had fallen in love with her. I consider that this was the moment when I had started rising in love with her.

However, still I wanted to be fully sure about her decision, her—"Yes, I do", because, it was possible that in front of her other family members due to fear and embarrassment, she could not have revealed her secrecy. (You know the super-hit film story of *Hum Dil De Chuke Sanam*! I did not want to be another Ajay Devagan or Salman Khan!) And therefore, I had written her a letter in which I had described about myself as honestly as possible and I had asked her—still, you want to marry me, please send your written confirmation. In that letter, I had also suggested her that if 'something' is hidden within you; please tell me, I might help you. I do not want to repeat the story of movie, *Hum Dil De Chuke Sanam* in my real life. So, at least, I can make free you from my side. However, because I was in love with her and whatever happens in a movie or love-songs—that was happening with me in reality, so I could not wait for her letter and telephoned her after one week. I asked her, have you received my letter? What have you decided now? She had received my letter and this time, her answer was bold and crisp but beautiful, "Yes! I want to marry you and only you! You listened to me or should I repeat it again and again…!" I said, "Yes, I listened to you. Thank you and it is my pleasure that you want to marry me."

And love is such a situation… it is difficult to describe this situation in words. Though, we both were fully sure that we were going to marry as soon as possible, but still we feared that we might be separated, and we could not bear this separation at any cost. There was not any obvious cause but still there was a fear. And really, this fear is very dangerous. In my experience; this is one of the most dangerous fears, because once you fall in love with someone (here, I think, fall is the correct word to describe this process!); you can never come out of it. At that time, I myself could not imagine to live my life without Priyanka. Really, I myself was surprised on my own position—how it can happen with me, but it had been happened. And therefore, to come out of this fear, I had decided to marry her as quickly as possible. Just within 6 months of love affair through letters and telephone, I decided to marry her. After that, with the consent of her parents (though my parents and especially my father were not fully agreed with my decision), I married her in a temple at Varanasi in May 2001… and this is my brief love-story!

I know there are not many ups-and-downs in this story, but you know that, a story-writer intentionally creates many ups-and-downs in cinema-story to make it more interesting. Otherwise, who will see such stories and how such people can earn crores of rupees! Really, at present, TV and cinema (entertainment industry) people are earning lots of money with their acting and dancing and others *latake-and-jhatke*!

Now, we again return to our original discussion, that is, what is fair in love? Friends, whatever may be the situation or circumstance; a true and sensible lover can never hate his lover. He can never be cruel with his lover. Love makes someone soft, sensitive and caring. Love has power to change a cruel-mind into a loving-soul. So, there is no place of hate and cruelty in love. Yes, I know and have experience that, it is difficult to bear the pain of separation from our lover. But if our lover wants to bear this pain, we can bear it—what is the other way! If she feels happy to see you in pain, let her feel happy. Even I was in love with Priyanka, if she had refused to marry me, I had accepted her refusal—not easily—but had accepted. Why she could have refused me—simple—to marry a better person who would be more handsome and richer than me. And though, I had this fear, in my first letter to her I had disclosed everything about me—it was not a love letter but a confirmation letter! In my letter, I had disclosed my qualification—we generally measure one's qualification with one's degrees and certificates; my monthly salary—nearly 5000 rupees; and my little property at village. However, even after knowing all these things, she agreed to marry me.

It proves that there are people in this world—even rich people, who cares honesty and sincerity. So, in case, Priyanka had refused to marry me, only because of her refusal, I could not start hating her. I might have started hating my own poorness and ordinariness, but not her—and I think this is the true meaning of love. In love, we may hate ourselves—our poorness and ordinariness, but not our lover. However, just hating oneself is not the solution of failing in love. One has to rise above and above to that level, where his soul and conscience can say, "You are not a poor and failure. You are rich, capable and unique." And at that moment, he starts feeling inner-peace and blessings from the Creator, which is the sole aim of one's life.

Besides, if caste and religious differences are creating hindrance in this matter, then I want to say that only science can solve this problem. Science clearly proves that there is no caste and religion of any elementary unit of mass and energy. Atoms and molecules have no caste and religion—no atom is Hindu or Muslim. An X-ray does not behave differently with people of different castes and religions. Oxygen gas does not make live people of only a certain caste and religion. So, science has done more than 90% job in eradication of caste and religious differences and discriminations. Now it is our job to understand science and apply this understanding in our real life so that we may overcome our false belief system. In fact, science has done the mind-job, and through this book, I want to do the heart-and-soul-job! I hope you can understand what I want to say.

Dating, Love, Marriage and Divorce: I have no experience of dating with girls and about love-affairs, so I cannot write anything about this mater. I have already mentioned above my love-experiences and love-story. Now, we proceed further to marriage and next to divorce. I must say that even in an arranged marriage, there must be a friendly conversation between the two individuals who are going to marry. Both individuals should discuss all those points which may affect their future-lives like their likes and dislikes, hobbies, family and financial and professional matters, their problems and difficulties, and other such issues/matters. They should be given enough time to discuss all these issues so that in future they may have very little differences.

Before my marriage, for nearly three months I have discussed many such issues through letters and on telephone with

Priyanka. Besides, all these issues can be discussed without "living-in" relation (also called 'trial marriage'). I am not against trial marriage, but if, at present, our parents and society are against it, we can little-bit manages with them. We should understand the situation and cooperate with our elders and society. Dear friends, in love or marriage relationship, first meet on the 'surface-level'—that is, on mind, thinking, behaviour and attitude, and then go for 'fusion' of your souls! I also experience that there is no other human relation in which, two human souls come to such a close-range as we come in a love or marriage relationship. Really, it is meeting and fusion of two souls. And therefore, before marriage, we must be sensible and considerate while selecting our life-partner, as we have to live one whole-life with her or him. However, if you fall in love with someone there is no question of selection, you must have to go with her or him. Your soul cannot be agreed to go with any other one. So, falling in love is a very different situation, and because I myself have gone through this situation, I have real experience of it.

Now, love and marriage part is over and we move forward and discuss the problems which we face after marriage. There are a lot of advices and suggestions in books and magazines to make a married-life successful. However, I consider that although one may be 100% cautious and careful in selecting his partner, one cannot be 100% sure about success of his married life! Marriage is nothing but just a friendly relation—of course, it is a unique and special relation, but more or less, it is also a friendship relation. And hence, like other friendship relations, it may also break at any point of time.

Sometimes and especially in the beginning years of my marriage, I and Priyanka had also quarreled a lot; but never reached to the point of divorce. Also, generally rich and upper class people go for divorce. Poor, ordinary and lower-middle class people rarely go for divorce. They quarrel—even bull-fight, but rarely they take divorce. They manage somehow or anyhow, but they manage! However, I must say that if in your living-in or marriage relation (or in any other relation), there is a totally unbearable-situation—you are always screaming and crying, living in stress and depression; then you must break that relationship instantly, or as soon as possible. There is no human relation which we cannot break. By nature, we are all free like an atom. Of course we are also bonded as atoms are bonded but if required, an atom makes itself free by detaching with other atoms. So, we should also behave like an atom. Every relation must have a mutual-understanding and friendly-attitude, only then that relation can survive, otherwise it cannot survive.

I myself treat everyone as a friend but if my counterpart or opponent is not interested to keep a friendly relation with me and seniority-complex comes in our relation, then I better like to break that relation. In the beginning of my life, as you know, I had broken relation even with God. I was a poor and ordinary person and people used to say—God is a very rich and great entity, we are like slaves and servants of God; so I had better liked to break relation with God. I can keep relationship with God only when God treats me as a friend and not as a poor and helpless person.

So, you can understand my thinking and attitude. I cannot simply stand like a beggar in front of God and start begging in the name of praying; no, never. So, respect yourself and live with dignity. We are just friends and if a couple is totally disagreed to live together with a friendly attitude, they must break that relation. When we die, at that time, our all relations are broken. So, if it is critically required we can break a married relation too—let happen whatever happens—who cares. I alone am not here to care. Everyone has to care. Also, we are friends and not servants or care-takers of others.

I do say, in modern age, no one should behave like Jesus; no one needs to be a Jesus. No one should be crucified like a Jesus—a lovely and innocent soul. Jesus—such a lovely soul; I have no word to describe him. I can only say to this soul—I love you… I have nothing more to say. So, no one needs to behave like a Jesus or Gandhi. We just need to be a human being—a friend.

Of course, I also know that in our married relation, if we break-up, other people and society will criticize us. In fact they are for this job!—gossip, rumor, *hai-hai... hi-hi!* Let them do their job. But just to avoid such criticism, we cannot live in stress and depression life-long. No, from my side, I have a BIG NO. Therefore, we must need all to be sensible and caring, only then we can create and develop a healthy family-relations. Remember, peace and happiness matter the most in our life, and if, being peaceful and happy is selfishness, then I say, be selfish! So, we need all to be sensible, friendly and caring, only then we can create a healthy family, society, India and world.

As we know, at present, divorce rate is very high. It started from modern countries, but now it has become a common practice in India. A few arguments or quarrellings on a certain issue, and a couple decide to live separately, they take divorce. Many couples are crying for divorce and have given petition in court for it. They are not ready to live with their life-partner—soul-mate. Before marriage or at the time of marriage, they promised to live together for seven lives but only in one life, they started crying! What would happen in their next six lives! They can only wish that this present married relation would be their seventh one!

My friends, this matter does not finish with jokes. This matter has a deep concern with our children's life and future. We should understand that our children deeply needed our love and care in their childhood and teenage. If we take divorce, it creates an adverse effect on their lives. So, to avoid this situation, I have a simple and sensible idea—you give birth to a child only when you both partners become 100% sure that you will not take divorce in future. To be fully sure, you may take time from one year to five years or even more. But, before being fully assured, do not produce any child. This decision is for better future of our children. If we have simple ways to avoid pregnancy, why should we spoil lives of our children? No, it is not fair. In fact, it is inhumanity. So, please stop this inhumanity. Otherwise, in your next birth, your turn will come to face this inhumanity! Be prepared to face that. Be aware—as you sow so shall you reap—this is the way of working of nature and existence, and no one can change it.

Female Feticide: Female feticide is a very serious issue not only in India but all over the world. On internet, we can study lots of data and analysis about this matter, however here, without putting any data to show its adverse effect on our society, I will discuss this issue in a simple and practical manner. First, why people abort a female baby before her birth? Very simple and straight reply—because people have a mind which thinks in a business-manner, that is, in a profit-and-loss manner and people see profit in male child and loss in female child. You may give 10 logics to avoid aborting female baby; but people will say—Ok, you give birth to 10 girls, why are you teaching and teasing me! Instead of giving logics and suggestions, do it practically. What will you say? Just shut-up! Our all human-relations have become a business matter. We want to gain profit in our every relation.

Another crucial reason is that, we want at least a male baby, and simultaneously we do not want more babies, as we have no money to make arrangements for more than one or two children, and therefore we abort female babies until we get a male baby. Thirdly, we know, and it is a reality too that, in future we may have to face such serious problems like sexual-assault, rape, and dowry-harassment with our daughter. So we better like to abort female babies.

These are down-to-earth realities and we cannot simply shut and turn our eyes from these realities. We can make laws to stop female feticide but simply making laws cannot overcome this problem. Even law-makers and law-implementers are law-breakers then how we can hope that others will follow their laws. No, we cannot hope; otherwise our hope will be proved futile.

Think in a practical way—why people want a female baby and not a male baby from their cow and buffalo! I think I do not need to explain it. This is so simple that even the most stupid person of this planet knows about it. In fact, from this book, if I remove all scientific facts, which I have modified with my understanding and awareness, then there will be nothing left in this book about which common people do not know.

Reality is that common people know everything—but due to lack of understanding and awareness, they know everything only with a business and money-mind and the result of this money-mind is in front of us. We are standing in-between different kinds of social evils and problems. Here, I have mentioned a very important point and all intelligent people like leaders and politicians, law-makers, administrators, social reformers etc. must note this point, and that point is—common people know about everything, but only with a clever and cunning business-mind—profit-loss, money, false-ego, prestige etc.; and this cunning business-mind can be corrected only with understanding and self-awareness and this I want to do by my writings.

Now, what will be the result if we continuously avoid female babies? Obviously, there will be shortage of girls? Female to male ratio will be highly decreased. Most of the men would remain unmarried. Prostitution and woman-trafficking will increase. And due to all these problems, in coming days, our family and social structure will be adversely affected. But the question is—who thinks and cares all these issues? Who has time to think about all these problems? It is India, here everything goes; *yahan sab kuchh chalata hai!* Am I right? Yes I am right!

Friends, we—especially government, leaders, laws-makers and their implementers should understand that this is not an individual's duty and responsibility to think about all these social issues. This is a social and total-humanity problem, so we should all think about these problems and do something for it.

However, present situation is not like this. Presently, an individual faces difficulties due to a girl child and not total society, leaders and law-makers. Society does not help in providing monetary help (dowry) to marry one's daughter. Even close relatives do not help a person, what to say about society people. Besides, society does not help when someone misbehaves or harasses or rapes someone's sister or daughter. On the contrary, society entertains such situations. People see such things as a real-life drama and create gossips and rumors about such matters. They find a good time-pass.

There are many people who go to cinema-hall to see these things, so they find a good opportunity free of cost in their surroundings. And, because of this very corrupt-mentality of common people, an individual takes such a decision to abort a female baby. A father and even a mother ignore all moral, social, ethical and traditional values and take such a cruel decision. It is also a fact that law-makers make only laws but they do not observe the ground realities, otherwise even after observing the ground realities, they ignore them. They simply give goody-goody moral and ethical ideas and make strict laws. But common people are not fools. They know very well that goody-goody ideas cannot feed their children. Goody-goody ideas cannot save their daughters from rape and sexual-assaults. They cannot save them from burning-alive for dowry.

People may not be educated, but they daily hear and see such incidents in their surroundings and also on TV. So, people know about ground realties very well. Again, even educated, sensible and urban people are aborting female babies so what to say about uneducated and rural people. Also, reality is that uneducated and poor people have no money for medical check-up to detect the gender of their baby and then for abortion (total minimum expenditure nearly ₹1500, and because it is illegal, so expenditure may go up to ₹5000 to 10000). So generally, poor people accept their every child as a God-gift! Even today, some of them have accepted 5-6 and even more such God-gifts! These people take God-gifts to spoil them! They give them poverty and hunger as birth-gift! So, basically, female-babies are aborted by urban and educated people and not by villagers and rural people. Really, situation is very critical. Illiterate and rural poor people are increasing population and hence increasing poverty and unemployment, and on the other side, educated and urban people are aborting female-babies and decreasing number of educated, intelligent and developed girls. So, our India is deteriorating by both of them.

Anyway, in this matter, my view is very simple and clear—after marriage, you give birth to 1 or 2 children without detecting their genders—even both happen to be girls, accept them, that's all. I accept my child in the same manner. I have no more money and hence till now I have only one child. When I will become a millionaire (I am trying to become a millionaire through KBC, but till now I have not got this great opportunity!), I will give birth to another child. In fact, as per my thinking, only rich and millionaires should produce two or even more than two children. A common man should produce only one child. Most importantly and as you know, I hate poverty the most. There are no words to describe my abhorrence for poverty. So, I can never give poverty to my children. My parents and grandparents may be fools but not I. So, I will try to give prosperity to my child to my level best but never poverty. And, I think if every person hates poverty as I hate it, I am sure we can eradicate poverty very soon from India and the world. We need a deep abhorrence towards poverty and save our children from poverty and unemployment, only then we can change India and world.

Regarding making strict laws, I would like to say that if law-makers make more strict laws, people would act in more cunning and corrupt ways. People will definitely find some ways to cheat strict laws, and money helps them to find their ways. Money is the biggest way-finder. It makes a way everywhere. Yes, occasionally we can find a culprit—1 in 100, and we can punish him, but 99 culprits are safe and these 99 culprits encourage and motivate others to do unsocial and illegal activities. And this is not true only in female-feticide case but it is true in all unsocial and illegal activities.

So, just making strict and stringent law is not enough. We need honest, sincere and sensible law-implementers, that is, honest and sincere police, lawyer and judge; only then we can correct and stop illegal and corrupt activities of people.

If government wants to save female babies, in my view, please start giving huge monetary help to those parents, especially poor parents, who give birth to a girl baby. At very birth of a girl baby, make deposit of rupees 50 thousand in her name for a period of 15-20 years. In addition, government should give other privileges to such people, like more subsidies on LPG gas and water-electricity charges. Girls, especially of poor family, should be given reservation in government jobs. They should be given free-passes in trains for appearing in competitive examinations. They should be provided free-education up to PhD. There are many such initiatives which government can take to increase the number of girls.

It is also possible that in future, due to shortage of number of girls, the demand of girls will increase and hence their value will increase—a simple economics-principle that if supply of an item decreases, its demand and value increases. So, at that time, a bride-parent may demand money (dowry) from bridegroom-parent! And this matter may again turn into a business deal and a new type of problem may be developed. Therefore, the only way to come out of all these problems is—be sensible and considerate, expand your thinking and view, and do your best for your child as well as for society and nation, that's all.

✌

5

Think, Self-Analyse and Decide-Yourself

Think, Self-Analyse and Be a Self-Director

Friends, think for a while: who teaches a tiny insect to move away from a hot or a cold area? Who teaches an ant to go towards a pill of sugar? Who teaches a magnet to attract or repel another magnet? Who teaches different atoms to react with one another? I know you know the answer, the answer is—there is no teacher for these natural bodies. In fact, every natural body acts by itself. It gets feelings and stimulation from within and takes action accordingly. Every natural body—tiny or tall, is free to act and move as per its own inbuilt virtue and potential.

We are also a natural body and we are also free to move and act as per our own inbuilt virtue and potential. We are free to move anywhere and act anything what we feel or want. However, to move in a right direction—the direction which leads us towards peace, happiness and satisfaction; we need a self-thinking, self-analysing and a self-judging power, which we get by regular practices in our life. They do not come to us in an hour or in a day; instead, they take time and practices. In addition, for this, we may need to leave readymade answers and beliefs of our past ancestors. I do not say that everything of our past generation is outdated and obsolete, but I must say that we need personally to check their reality and credibility. Only then our thinking and awareness can be developed.

Only because of my thinking and self-analysing power, I have written these many things in my books—otherwise I am also very common man like you. I am not a genius or God-gifted but my problem is—I do not think even the greatest intelligent person of the world as a genius or God-gifted! I consider him as a common man. I read and understand him considering him as common man. I read either Gautama Buddha or Sri Krishna or I read Albert Einstein or Isaac Newton; but I read all of them considering them as common man. What is right and what is wrong—I think in my own way. I do not depend on others advices and decisions. Let it be a decision of a leader, scientist, guru or a god, but I can easily reject it if it does not suit with my thinking. And I strongly feel to say that this should be the way of thinking of every Indian—especially of youth of India.

Again, it is possible that we may be wrong in our thinking and we may do mistakes—so what, we will learn from our mistakes and correct them. We will not stick with our mistakes rubbing our hands in stress and disappointment, but we will proceed further correcting our mistakes. Therefore, think, self-analyse and act in your own way to change and develop India. If we all make effort to change and develop India, we can definitely change it very soon and fulfill the dream of our beloved president Dr. Abdul Kalam—Vision2020.

Follow Your Inner-Conscience and Not a Leader or a Guru: Friend, when there is no role-model or leader in the atomic and molecular world or any other natural world, then how there can be any role-model, leader or guru in the human world. If an atom or molecule does not follow any other atom or molecule then why we should follow others? More importantly, if we follow others, then what will happen to our own understanding and intelligence—which we have acquired by birth? How can we develop our own thinking and awareness, if we continue believing and following others? No, we can't.

Therefore, we must use our own brain to understand and experience the reality of a matter. Everyone has a soul, and awareness is the basic virtue of a soul; so we must use this virtue of our soul. Only by using this virtue we can develop it, otherwise we cannot develop it. Therefore, instead of believing and following others, we should think ourselves and listen to our own inner-feelings. In our inner-feelings, there is a little-voice which guides us in our life. Listening to one's inner-feelings and moving accordingly is the sign of an awakened and intelligent soul.

Friends, remember, with mind, we may catch various thoughts and ideas from different sources like books, schools, teachers, gurus, etc., but these all theories and ideas cannot make us intelligent, creative, talented, and developed. The reason behind is—a theory or an idea stimulates only our mind but not our inner-core, our feelings, our soul. Our soul gets stimulation and activation only by self thinking and analysing and self-effort. From the ancient history, there have been many great people, who have made effort for development of people and society, but most of them have been proved unsuccessful—why, only because, we lack self-thinking and self-effort. People simply keep theories of books in their minds but do not utilize the 'insight' hidden behind those theories. They know verbally a lot of things—they become graduates and post-graduates, but they know matters as parrot knows—only verbal. In such a poor situation, it is clear that only by self thinking and analysing and self-effort we can develop ourselves and our society and nation.

No Fate and God-Gift—only Our Sincere-Efforts Make Us Talented: If we see someone virtuous, creative and talented, we think that this is a matter of God and God-gift, or it is matter of fate and destiny. However, reality is that virtue and creativity are not a matter of God-gift, fate and destiny, but it is a matter of inner-passion and sincere effort to fulfill our passion. Otherwise, if we consider this matter from a spiritual point of view then this matter is related with the crystallization of our soul. In fact, the person who seems a God-gifted has already made effort to crystallize his soul and hence he has developed his inbuilt virtue in his very past life. In modern science age, you may think that the matter of pre-and-post life is an absurd theory of spirituality, however remember that, science has not yet proved that we are just a mixture of sex-cells!

Study the latest theory of science about this matter, and you will find that science has not yet completed its investigation in this matter. Science itself accepts that it has very little findings and knowledge in this matter and it is still investigating this matter. So, until science completes its investigation, do not think that life is just a developed-form of two sex-cells. No, in fact, in my consideration, life is a virtuous-chemistry of nature and existence, and we are all a part of this chemistry. So experience this chemistry and make effort to give a better product through this chemistry.

How we develop and become creative, here I have explained this matter with some real-life examples: friend, in this birth, if you have no curiosity and interest in science and technology, and if you dream that in your next birth you would become a doctor, engineer or a scientist; then only you dream-God can do such a miracle but not the real-God. Similarly, at this time, if you are not even a bathroom singer and you dream that in your next birth you would become a famous singer; then only your dream-God can do such a miracle but not the real-God. However, sorry to say that such a magical and miracle dream-God is only a dream but not reality. Reality is only this nature and existence about which I have already mentioned lots of things and you have also studied these things in your school text books. So, I do not need to fill pages of this book describing Physics, Chemistry, Biology and other branches of science. That is, I do not need to describe Force, Work and energy, Newton's laws of motion, Solar-system, Ecosystem, Photo-synthesis, Reproduction, Atoms and molecules, Chemical reactions etc… etc. No, you have already studied these things.

I have nothing to describe anything more about nature and existence—the real God. I have not found any new theory about nature to teach you. Yes…one thing I must say that if you have not understood these subjects properly and clearly, you should again read those school text-books to understand them clearly. I myself have revised all these things while teaching my child at home. In fact, I had started studying from 5th standard (—how, I have explained later), so I needed to study the basics again.

Further, here I have mentioned only few examples of art, talent, creativity and intelligence like being a doctor, scientist or a singer; however, as you know, there are many fields and dimensions of art, creativity and intelligence. But in every field, the matter is same. It means, in every field, we need curiosity, self-interest, self-motivation, and most importantly self-effort—a sincere effort. These are the basic ingredients of art, talent, creativity, intelligence, and self-development.

This existence is creating, nurturing, developing, and organizing our all art and creativity through us. The existence does not bless anyone with art and creativity, but it motivates us, induces us from within, to make effort to express our inherent art and creativity. One who listens to his inner-voice makes effort and remaining people just move behind money, power, prestige, fun and entertainment.

Furthermore, art and creativity are natural processes and they are very delicate and sensitive processes. They need time and effort. They do not happen in a magical way—within a moment an egg turns into a hen… no, a natural process does not take place in this way. It takes time and effort. Just to make a simple bulb, Edison had taken three years! Edison… who is considered a genius! He had succeeded to make a bulb after so many ways-of-thinking, experiments, efforts and failures!

Therefore, if you want to do something or become something, you must start doing that thing at this very moment. Only then, one day, you will become that something, you will fulfill your dream; otherwise you will always remain desirous and dreaming. Like a pendulum, you will move between the two ends of life—birth and death. Most of the people of this planet are moving between these two ends, and they are creating unnecessary burden of population on this planet. And sadly, most of them are from India! If you are one of them, come out of this mob with your self-thinking and effort.

Friends, it is a simple logic that if there is a God and He has gifts, He will certainly give His gifts to everyone. He cannot be biased and unfair with us, and if He is biased, we cannot call Him a God. A biased and unfair body should be better called a fraud and corrupt-body but not God. And, with my own experience I know that we have a God who is fair, lovely, caring and compassionate, and that God is our creator-existence. So, our God has given some gift to everyone, but it is the individual's responsibility to feel and recognize his inner-gift.

Additionally, it is the individual's responsibility to make an effort to emerge his inner-gift—his inner-virtue. God has not hands like us to draw and bring-out our inbuilt art and virtue.

No, our God is handless—and I am not feeling good saying God as handless, because who we are—we are all hands of God! India has 240 crores of hands and if we consider whole humanity then God has nearly 15 billion hands! So, we are the working hands of God and whatever God does, He does through us. God motivates us through our inner-feelings to move, act and work. Therefore, we should come out of this false belief that some people are God-gifted and remaining people are Without-God-gifted. No, we are all God-gifted but we need inner-search and inner-effort to find and develop our inner virtue. If we cannot do this; sorry, God is helpless, God can do nothing.

What is Virtue and Creativity?: It is somewhat a difficult thing to define virtue and creativity; however we can understand this matter with this simple analogy: the virtue and creativity of a human being is like the fragrance of a flower; and as we know that we cannot define fragrance of a flower. We can only experience it and for that, we need to go in a practical way—we inhale the fragrance of a flower and then we experience its flavour and sweetness, and that is the actuality of its fragrance. Similar is the case with human virtue and creativity. Only after absorbing the music of a musician we can experience its melody and sweetness and that is the creativity of that musician.

Further, we should be aware that the mechanism, which works behind the emerging of fragrance of a flower, the same mechanism works behind the emerging of creativity of a human being. As fragrance of a flower emerges due to natural-process occurring at its core; similarly, the virtue and creativity of a human being emerges due to natural-process happening at one's core (soul). Both are natural bodies and hence their internal mechanism works in a similar manner.

However, there is a difficulty with a human body and that difficulty arises due to our SP-oriented mind (SP means—Success, Status, Security, Power, Property, Prestige etc.). We mostly think and act according to our SP-oriented mind and hence our potential-virtue, which is coiled-up within our core, does not get an opportunity to emerge. Secondly, due to habit of our easy-way-going and lack of courage for taking risk, our soul is not strong enough to crack the shield of our SP-oriented mind and emerges its virtue. Therefore, we need inner-energy and crystallization so that our soul may crack this shield and emerges our virtue.

Why Do We Have Difference In Our Virtue and Intelligence?: Medical science finds that we are all made up of the same basic materials. We are all made up of same atoms, cells, tissues, bones, flesh, and vital organs. Not only this, medical science finds that even our brain cells are made up of the same cells. It means, on material level even a scientist's brain is similar to an illiterate's brain. And in fact, due to this very similarity, many parts of our body like eyes and kidney can be transplanted—interchanged. Thus, on mass level, we do not find any significant difference among ourselves. We are all same.

Then, this question naturally rises that where is that difference due to which we have difference in our awareness, intelligence and creativity; and the answer is—that difference is at our core, at our energy level, that is, at soul-level. Due to difference in crystallization of our soul, there is difference in our thinking-level, awareness, creativity and intelligence. And, due to the same difference, there is difference between the brain (intelligence) of a scientist and that of an illiterate. Therefore, we should all make effort to crystallize our soul, and develop our knowledge and awareness, only then we can develop a virtuous and healthy India.

What Is the Real Cost of Virtue and Creativity?: Today, we have nearly all luxury and comforts like AC, PC, car, laptop, airoplane, mobile etc. to enjoy our life in a comfortable manner. In past, we had only dreams of these things—a paradise dream, but now this dream has become reality.

However, have you ever thought how this dream became reality? Have you ever thought what the actual costs of these luxury-comforts are? For instance—have you ever thought what the actual cost of a bulb is? We just spend rupees 15 and buy a bulb—is this the actual cost of a bulb? No, absolutely not. Just 15 rupees can never be the actual cost of the sincere efforts of Thomas Alva Edison. For making this bulb, he had put his sincere efforts for three years, so how can we pay for his efforts just by paying rupees 15. In fact, we can never pay for his actual efforts—because, even with the whole money of the world we could have never been able to make a bulb. So, a bulb is incredible—no price can be justified for it.

However, there is a way to pay for his sincere and incredible efforts and that is—our gratitude and thankfulness towards him. Yes, just our genuine thankfulness towards Edison and all such people is the genuine cost of their creative and incredible efforts. These people need only our sincere thankfulness and nothing more than that. In fact, in my awareness, these people are the real leaders of humanity. Leader means a person who leads others with his virtue and vision—who gives some light like the 'bulb' of Edison to move forward.

A leader is not a leader who pulls or pushes others in a use and throw manner with his power and force like most of the present politicians and leaders usually do. Such politicians and leaders should be better called PPP (Public-Pullers-and-

Pushers) but not leaders. In fact, looking the present scenario of politics of India, politicians should be better called poly-trick-cians but not leaders, as they mostly play tricks with public to win election. They think only about vote-bank and how to remain in power. They are not genuinely interested to develop people and society—to develop India as a developed country. However, leaders and politicians must be cautioned that no one can play trick with God—the creator-existence. We must pay for our wrong doings—in one way or the other way. God is not going to leave anyone. We must reap our sowing—it is 100% sure.

Anyway, I have already discussed a lot of things about cheating, frauds and corruption and about their causes and cure in my earlier chapter, so now I do not feel to elaborate it any more. In fact, in my writings, I want to focus on good and virtuous things and not bad and corrupt things. So, we should see the valuable and incredible effort of incredible people like Edison, Newton, Einstein etc.; and inspiring from these people, we should make effort to bring some light-and-delight on this earth. This book is also a little-effort from my side. So friends, wherever you are and whoever you are, you make a little effort from your side, and certainly with our collective little-efforts we can change India, and if possible, world too.

Passion Is More Important than Knowledge and Mind: People, in general, think that mind plays a great role in success and development of a person. They think that only with a better knowledge (mind), a person can be a successful one. However, this is not the actual reality. In fact, in a human body, the real virtuous and intelligent entity is one's soul and not his mind. The root source of virtue and creativity is not in one's thinking and knowledge, but it is in the action in the guidance of his inner feelings and soul. We have to feel the fragrance of our inner art and virtue and make effort to emerge it.

As a matter of fact, this is the reason that modern-science does not find a direct relation between creativity and mind. Many times, science finds a contradictory relation between mind and creative-intelligence. It finds that some creative and intelligent people are not good in text-books' knowledge but they are fantastic in thinking and creativity. Even today, many creative and genius people of past age are famous for their poor memory. So, the actual reason behind this contradiction is—such people have a great passion and zeal to make effort continuously. Otherwise, from knowledge and thinking point of view they are as normal as we are.

Therefore, we must come out of this misconception that only a knowledgeable and intellectual person can be a creative and intelligent one. No, everyone can be a creative and intelligent person with his inner-passion and zeal. Hence, search and research your soul and feel your inner virtue and passion and make effort to emerge it. Accumulating more power, property, and prestige—3P is not the sole aim of our life, instead emerging our virtue and being peaceful and blissful is the sole aim of our life. Existence has created us for it.

Everyone Has an Inbuilt-Creative Power: If you have read science, you know that even a tiny atom has some virtues and characteristics. Every atom is unique. So there must be some virtues and characteristics in every human being as a human being is made up of trillions and trillions of atoms. In fact, with a simple analogy, a human being should be trillions times more virtuous than an atom! Therefore, it is 100% sure that every person has some art and virtue. Now, how one can recognize his art and virtue?

There is no other sure-way except recognizing oneself one's art and virtue. Others can observe your art and virtue, they may give suggestion to express them, but only you yourself can feel their intensity and make effort to express them.

On this planet, there have been many simple and ordinary people who have become great and genius only because of their inner-passion and sincere-effort. These people prove that everyone has an inbuilt virtue—either in a developed-form (in case of a strong and crystallized-soul), or in a seed-form (in case of a developing-soul). So, until one feels one's inner virtue and self-determine and makes effort to express it, no one can help him. Teacher, guru and mentor etc. have a very little role in it. So, no matter what you are today, try to become what you want to become tomorrow, and start doing that thing right now.

A teacher, guru, mentor, writer etc. can only explain this matter as I have explained it above, but no one can bring-out your potential-virtue from your core—it is sure. You yourself have to make effort for it. You can read hundreds of books about this matter—motivational, inspirational, spiritual, philosophical, religious, self-help, self-development, psychology etc., and you can take guidelines of hundreds of teachers and gurus, but until you self-determine and make effort, no guru or book can help you. Even God cannot help you what to say about a guru or a book. However, in present corrupt and commercial age, there are many fake and phony teachers and gurus who can assure you that you need not to worry about this matter. You just leave it to them; they have special divine-power to develop you. However, such all assurances and promises are false and bogus. Never believe such fake and phony teachers and gurus.

Many great awakened souls like Sri Krishna, Gautama Buddha, Jesus, Guru Nanak and many others had not been succeeded in awakening and developing common men only because of lack of self-determination and self-effort of common men.

Most of the common men want everything readymade. From food to knowledge and from entertainment to enlightenment—everything should be readily available. Just click a button and item should be served. This readymade-attitude is the biggest obstacle in the development of people and humanity. We must leave this readymade-attitude and we should all put our sincere effort for our development. Just do your best and leave rest to the creator existence (the real God). The creator existence has its own intelligence and awareness to judge our sincerity and effort. Remember, success is not in our hand but effort is certainly in our hand, and the creator existence has given us birth only for making effort and not for being a successful or a winner.

Be a Realist and Not a Dreamer: It is great surprise that even in the modern science age, people think in a 'be-positive' manner. People think that by being positive and hopeful, they can solve their problems. At least, they can hope that their problems will be solved one day or the other day. However, by being-positive or being-negative, one can never solve his problem; instead only by effort with understanding one can be able to solve his problem. An optimist or a be-positive person is nothing but a day-dreamer. He dreams for a heaven and luxury but lives in hell and misery. There are many people in this world (and sadly, most of them are Indians), who are living in misery but they dream for luxury. And at the end of their life, they die in hell blaming their poor fate and destiny. This is the real life-stories of most of the people of this world. Therefore friends, instead of being positive or negative you be a realist.

Understand that nature is neither positive nor negative, but it is both. The basic elementary particle of nature, that is, an atom is neither positive nor negative, but it is both, and hence it is free, stable and independent. A positive particle like a proton or a negative particle like an electron is not free and stable, but an atom having all proton, electron and neutron is free and stable. Certainly, an atom is situational; means, momentarily it becomes positive, negative or neutral. It moves, acts and reacts with other atoms to give a better product and to gain more stability, but comparing to a single proton or an electron, an atom is more stable, free and independent. We are also a natural body made up of atoms and hence we should also behave like an atom. It means, momentarily, we may be positive, negative or neutral, but overall, we should be always free, stable and independent.

A realist person is that who understands himself in a practical manner. He understands his strength as well as his limitations, and understanding these factors, he sets his goal accordingly. He does not dream like most of the dreamy people who live in hell and finally die in it blaming their poor fate and destiny. Instead of blaming others, he makes effort to reach his goal and he knows only one thing that only making effort is in his hand. Result is not in his hand—it is in fact not in even God's hand, because God is not his enemy but his friend, his care-taker and supporter. So, if he is not getting his result, it means he needs to make more efforts. And, this whole teaching has been taught by Lord Sri Krishna thousands of years back. But, it is of no use. Still, people think more about result than making efforts.

Money, power, status etc. are more important than making effort to get them; otherwise, people use shortcuts to get them. Besides, it is also a ground reality that people and society do not see our efforts; they see only results—our bungalow, car, money, power, post and status. And this money, power and status seeking mentality bring cheating, fraud and corruption in our society—but who cares! So, for all such social evils and problems, not only police, judges and leaders are responsible but we are all responsible. And we know very well that just making stringent laws and orders cannot solve these problems. So, at present, we have stood in a very critical and choked situation and we need all to make effort to come out this choked situation, only then we can take breath in the fresh air of humanity.

Therefore friends, stop dreaming for money, power and status and make effort to get what you actually want—what your soul wants. Dream and desire are not going to fulfill our wants; instead they will bring only disappointment, despair and finally death, and again rebirth for doing the same job, that is, dreaming, desiring, disappointment... and then death; and this cycle continues. Hence, break this cycle, be a sensible and realist person, and put your best effort to satisfy your soul's desires and dreams. I have done and still I am doing the same thing in my life, and I feel that though I am an ordinary person, I am one of the most satisfied and peaceful person in the world. Anyone in this world can check my satisfaction and peacefulness level.

More importantly, please do not think about being a success or a failure, you just put your sincere effort. Only your sincere effort will make you peaceful, satisfied and blissful—even without getting success or result. If we consider in a practical way, then even great people like Sri Krishna, Gautama Buddha, Jesus, Nanak and Kabir etc. are failures; how, because they failed to get their required result. Their aim was to bring peace, love, brotherhood and friendliness among us; but seeing poverty, hatred, violence and misery in the present world, we can easily say that they have failed in getting their required result.

Still we people are fighting, quarreling and murdering one another. We are ready for third world war. This shows that such great and god-men are failures rather 'great' failures! But, at the same time, it is also true that these people are the most peaceful and blissful people in the world, and this is only because of their sincere effort. Therefore, leave thinking about being a success or a failure; you just put your best and sincere effort.

Only Hard-Work Is Not Enough!: Often we hear that we must do hard-work to be a successful person. Hard work is the basic key of all success. Nearly all successful people describe this charming word in their success-story. However, to be a successful person in a genuine sense, the first and foremost thing we need is—recognizing our inner art and virtue and making sincere effort to bring it out. Our sincere effort may look as hard-work to others, but the individual who makes efforts, knows that he does not do hard work, but he just makes effort to express his art and virtue. For example, in my wife's eyes, I do hard work for my writing—after office work, at evening and night, I study books and magazines; sometimes I also ignore to teach my son and for that my wife scolds me; again waking-up at night between 2 and 3 am and writing for 3-4 hours (it is my most preferable time for writing). So, in her eyes, I do hard work for my writing, but the problem is, I cannot show her the peace, satisfaction and happiness that I get due to my writing—there is no way to show her. I cannot show her blessings of creator-existence (God) that I get by my writing—that only I can feel.

Friends, think for a while—without knowing, in which direction and dimension you want to move to be a successful person, how can you work hard in that direction? First, we have to feel the direction—our inner virtue, art and passion—only then we can move in that direction wholeheartedly. And, moving or working in such a way, we do not feel that we are working hard, instead we feel that we are meeting the 'aim' of our life—for which this existence has created us. We feel very calm, peaceful and delightful. Here, I have shared my own experiences and with my own experience, I can say that same thing happens with every virtuous and creative soul.

For instance, same thing happens with a genuine singer—a born-singer. If a singer feels that he is working hard for singing, then he is not a born-singer. He is not born for singing. If one does not feel inner satisfaction and joyfulness while singing, my friendly suggestion to him is that he should stop singing and start searching 'within' to feel what his soul really wants to do? Only his soul, his inner-feelings can tell him what he should really do. Only his soul can give him power and determination to do his virtuous work, and his soul will make him so determined that no one can change his aim.

Certainly, in present professional and commercial age, most of the people choose a field where there is more money, power and prestige, but a strong and determined-soul never changes his aim and direction for money, power and prestige. In fact, due to the same strength and determination, there have been many virtuous, creative and visionary people on this earth. These people, for their efforts, have not thought about getting more money, power and status, but they have thought about progress and development of people and society and total humanity. They have thought about making this world a healthy and a beautiful place.

Therefore, inner-feeling, inner-search and inner-passion are the first and foremost requirements to be a successful person—a truly developed person. And about success, here I would like to quote the great words of one of the greatest scientists of the world—Albert Einstein. At one place, he has said—try not to become a success, rather try to be a man of values. This inspiring quotation of Albert Einstein has deeply inspired me. This single quotation proves that Albert Einstein was not only a great scientist but also a great human being, a great man of values. In my view, about success what Albert Einstein says is absolutely right, and through my writing, I am making an effort for the same purpose.

Kill the Problems but Never Kill Yourself: It is a great surprise that though human being is considered as the most intelligent being on this planet, it is the only being who commits suicide! Perhaps committing suicide is also a type of intelligence!! I know, today, committing suicide is a very big and serious issue of our society but I also know that whatever may be the issue, problem or difficulty, the solution of every problem is only one, and that is, making effort with sensibility to solve the problem. There is no other way except this. Simply quitting life by committing suicide is easy but it does not show sensibility and intelligence, instead it shows weakness and cowardliness of a human being.

We daily hear such news that someone committed suicide due to his poverty, unemployment, crops-failure, and other personal and social causes like—dowry, rape, sexual harassments, getting failure in competitive exams, cheating and fraud in love or in marriage relationship, etc… etc…; it is long list. However, in my experience, committing suicide is one of the most disgusting acts of a human life. A person, who commits suicide, wants to declare that this creator-existence is bad, its creation is bad, and in fact everything is bad. There is nothing good in this existence. But this poor thinking is only because of lack of sensibility and inner-awakening.

Of course, I agree that our parents, family, society, systems, government, leaders and other people are somewhat responsible for our difficulties and misery, but the question is, can quitting life by committing suicide change them? Daily, in India, at least 5-10 people commit suicide, but who changes—no one. Parents and families cry for few days and then life goes on…who cares! So, before committing suicide, you must think in a sensible manner.

Friends, I would like to ask everyone that—what is that most valuable thing, which you want to get and in case you failed to get it, you would decide to quit life. Otherwise, what is that most valuable thing which you already have, and in case you lost it, you would decide to commit suicide. You would break the journey of your growth in the middle of it. Because, I do not see any such a valuable thing for which I could commit suicide. Nothing is more valuable than my life. I can leave everything except my life. And, in case, if I face a problem, and as you know, as a common man like you, I also face problems. I have already faced problems of poverty and unemployment, which, in my experience, are the biggest problems of our society and humanity. So, if I face a problem, I try my best to kill or solve the problem. I do not know I will succeed or not, but I give my best to kill the problem.

It is also possible that I may be killed in killing the problem—it is other issue, but I can never kill myself with my own hand. And I strongly feel to say the same thing to you—to especially youths of India: kill the cause or problem which is killing you but never kill yourself. The problem may be anything; but I will say the same thing to you. From getting food to getting enlightenment (God), there are many problems, but whatever may be the problem, I will say same thing to you. You try your best to kill or solve the problem but never kill yourself.

Someone may ask me—have I ever thought about committing suicide? Unfortunately, my answer is yes! I have once thought about it. At that time I was nearly 23 years old, and at that moment, I was at a railway station, Sasaram (near Bodh-Gaya), Bihar. I was returning to my village (a small place named 'Majhouli' in Rohtas district of Bihar) after appearing in a competitive exam for a secured job. For a moment, I had thought to jump on the railway-track in front of a coming train! But I had thought it only for a moment, in the next moment I was laughing at my thought! I was surprised thinking that—oh! I can also think about committing suicide! Really poor and disgusting! And what was the basic cause of this thinking—my poverty and unemployment. I had been already proved a failure to become an engineer, it was frustrating me, but anyhow I manage it. However, nearly five years had been gone appearing in exams for jobs, but still I was a failure to get a secured job. At that time, after completion of fire sub-officer training, I was working at Oswal Chemical and Fertilizer Ltd, Paradeep, Orissa. But that job was a contract-job and you know the future of a contract job. So, basically, my poverty and unemployment were the main causes for my thinking to commit suicide. But, this incident had happened only for a moment, in the next moment I was ready to fight and kill my poverty and finally I killed it!

Due to scarcity of government jobs, common men generally say that getting a government job is like getting God; but I want to tell them that you people are totally mistaken. I have never made effort to get or meet God. Instead, I had always discarded God; however see—God himself came to meet me. So, getting God is so easy, even you hate and discard God deeply; God will repeatedly come to meet you and ask you, "Still you hate me? Am I really so bad?" and a day will come in your life, like it came in my life, when you will say to God, "No, I don't hate you. I love you. I am sorry, forgive me." Friends, God is not bad, we just need to change our view and perception about God; only then we can understand Him correctly.

Friends, poverty and unemployment had taken me at the door of death—as due to these problems, I had thought about committing suicide, and therefore, in revenge, I want to take them at the door of death. Yes, I want to finish poverty and unemployment from India and this world. I just need your help and support—I need your thinking and understanding. Just think in my way and then see how poverty and unemployment are eradicated from India in a few years. India will be totally changed. It will become a rich and prosperous country. And not only India, if every person of this world thinks in my way—this world can be changed. This world will become a good, rich and a prosperous place.

Friends, committing suicide is the most disgraceful act of human life, because it is disgracefulness towards the creator-existence—the God. It is an insult to the awareness, intelligence and compassion of God. Dear, this is the same intelligent and awareness existence about which the great scientist Albert Einstein has once said, 'I am a tiny drop of the ocean-of-intelligence'; and Isaac Newton has said, 'I am a small child playing with sands on the beach of ocean-of-knowledge'.

So our God—this existence, is highly intelligent, sensible, and responsive. Consider this: just to find a simple particle of existence—Higgs-Boson (also known as God-particle), all top-level scientists of world worked for nearly 14 years and still the particle is not fully examined. Still this matter is under investigation.

So our God is highly intelligent and responsible and He is working with a deep level plan. We can never measure His total intelligence, awareness and plan. Hence, by committing suicide, don't insult the awareness and intelligence of God. Whatever may be the situation or problem, put your best effort to solve your problem. You may be proved failure in solving your problem—I agreed; even then you never go for committing suicide. Take your failure as a lesson for your life. It will be bitter in taste, I know, but taste it—taste it thinking that you will never take birth again to taste it. I myself do not want to taste poverty and unemployment again in my future births, and therefore, I want to eradicate them totally from India and the world.

Friends, it is possible that you and I may be proved wrong in our thinking and planning, but this creator-existence which has created people like Einstein, Newton and Edison; and on the other side, people like Jesus, Sri Krishna, Gautama Buddha, Guru Nanak, and Kabir, cannot be proved wrong. Our creator has a deep-level plan for development of one and all and it is working on its plan day and night—a real worker of timing 24X7! So, our creator is very sensible, loving and caring; it is only we, who are careless and ignorant. Therefore, we should increase our understanding, sensibility and awareness so that we can understand and experience the love and care of our creator.

Friends, in spite of my strong friendly request, if you have still decided to commit suicide, then I suggest (and request too) you to wait a little more time to commit suicide! You wait until 45 to 50 years of your age! Whatever may be the situation, never commit suicide before this age. Why I am saying this—because, it is possible that today you may be a big failure and a very miserable person, but tomorrow you may be a great success and a happy soul. It is not a hope or a dream (in fact, I hate hope and dream, I rarely dream at night) but it is a reality—it is the reality of many great people.

Read biographies of many great and successful people, most of them are painful and full of grief. And, understand that by saying this; I do not want to say that poverty and struggle make a man great and successful. No, it is not poverty and struggle but it is one's endurance, will-power and continuous-effort that make a man great and successful. Moreover, a person becomes great by solving or at least making an effort to solve big problems like eradication of hatred and violence, misery and poverty from this world.

People like Gautama Buddha and Gandhi are great because they have tried to solve big problems. So, think a little above your personal problems, only then we can change India and the world. Therefore, I am sure that with your continuous effort, one day you must be able to solve your little personal problems like your poverty and unemployment etc. I have been succeeded to solve them so why not you—surely you can. I am also a common man like you.

Finally, friends, as a matter of fact, have you ever thought what happens after death or after committing suicide—whether one dies forever after committing suicide, whether one totally finished? Since, you do not know the reality of life-science, you commit this mistake; otherwise you can never commit this mistake. A sensible and awakened being can never commit this mistake. No doubt, by committing suicide, you would get a sudden-pain and then relief, but you should know that this relief is not permanent; it is very temporary in nature. It is of short-period. If you die in stress and depression, the nature will bounce you back quickly to release your stress and depression. Every action has a similar reaction—this follows everywhere.

Nature and existence have their own plan and they work according to their own plan. They do not work according to our silly and stupid thinking and plan, and committing suicide is the most stupid thinking—it is not a plan, so it is silly to write it as a plan. Therefore, be courageous and bold to face challenges. Ups and downs come in everybody's life. We should face them and make some way-out, but committing suicide can never be a way. It is a blockage and obstacle in our journey of life. Therefore friends, whatever may be the situation, cause, problem or difficulty; you put your best effort to solve it. If you succeeded, it is Ok; otherwise just hands up and say, I cannot solve it.

Prime ministers, presidents, top world-class leaders and scientists, geniuses, and even God are not able to solve every problem of the world, so who am I…, I am also a failure like these VIPs! So, don't be so serious—a little dance, song, music, fun and entertainment make our life more easy and comfortable. Hence, be determined, dedicated and sincere, but never too-serious to commit suicide. If thought comes to your mind to commit suicide—have a laugh on your thought as I had once laughed! Life is basically for enjoy—this is the full-form of life—see every letter of L-I-F-E and you will get the meaning!

Make Possible What Is Possible: Friends, every natural body has some virtues as well as some limitations. From tiny atom to large black-hole, everybody has some virtues as well as some limitations. We are also a natural body and we have also some virtues and some limitations. It is not a matter of luck, fate and destiny (as we usually believe-in so) but it is a matter of nature's virtue and potential. No doubt, some well known thinkers and philosophers have quoted some striking and thought-provoking quotations like 'nothing is impossible', 'The word impossible is found in the dictionary of fools' etc., however reality is that, even for science, everything is not possible, and science knows this reality very well.

Even for science, there are many things which are impossible and they will always remain impossible. For example, there is a famous principle in science which has the key word 'impossible', and that principle is, Heisenberg's Uncertainty Principle. This principle clearly states that it is impossible to determine the exact location and momentum of an electron at the same time. If we try to find one thing correctly (either location or momentum), the other thing becomes totally uncertain, even 100% uncertain. Therefore, it is totally phony to say, 'Nothing is impossible'. But I do say that we must make effort to make possible what is possible and most of our human, social, national and international problems are solvable. It is possible to solve problems like illiteracy, poverty, unemployment, corruption, violence, and injustice and discriminations in the name of caste, class, religion and gender. We just need making effort with understanding and sincerity.

6

To and For Young-Indians

Take Care of Your Child – India Will Naturally Change

Observing the poor and miserable condition of most of the children of India, it is clear that we are very careless and negligent towards growth and development of our children. I myself had lived like an orphan in my childhood. My father had remembered that he had a child only when I had grown up 13 years old! Before that he had forgotten me and his family. At 13 years of my age, he had brought me to Jamshedpur, admitted in a government school and took care of my studies. But again, he had left me after 10+2. He could not bear the expenditure of my studies.

Looking all these difficulties and problems, I want to say in a straight way to every Indian and especially to youth that, if you have no money for food and studies of your child—please don't give birth to him. I have said the same thing to my parents and also to my grandfather (grandmother had died when I was only 10 years old). Here, some people may reason that God gives birth to a child and not parents. I want to say these people, leave God and first take care of your child. Also, reality is that, more than 80% people of India have not that level of awareness to understand and experience the real God. Moreover, we should understand that God does not give only children. God gives many things like art, talent, virtue, creativity, awareness, intelligence etc., so why are we taking only children? Take art, virtue, talent and creativity; take awareness and intelligence; and also take money and wealth before giving birth to a child! It is stupidity to take only children from God and spoil their lives.

So, every parent has to take responsibility of his child. If you simply blame God and government, then you are simply spoiling lives of your children. No one is going to listen to your complaints. Your all complaints will be proved futile. Leader and politicians need your votes and not complaints and you also know this fact. Of course, God cares everyone but we also need to understand God's thinking and planning. God wants to develop everyone but we are so selfish that we do not care even our children. We spoil their lives just to fulfill our desires. We must leave this selfish attitude and we must care our children. We have to take care of basic needs of our children, and their health and education—only then we can change India. Our children are future of India and only by developing our children we can change future of our country.

Observing the miserable position of India regarding development of children of poor and underprivileged, it is clear that God, government and leaders have been proved failure. Though I am a government employee and I should not speak against government, but reality is in front of us and we are all seeing it. So, now this responsibility comes to the common men, and especially to youths of India, to take care of their children and change the future of India.

I know the youths of India have capability to take this responsibility. Yes! We can change the future of India and we have to do it at any cost. Even someone of us need to go in politics, we will go there—I myself am ready to go anywhere. But, keep in mind that we will go in politics to work and change India and not just for money, power and status as most people do. The least thing that we all have to do is—we have to take care of our children.

We don't have to give them born-poverty. We don't have to leave them to-die or remain-alive on their fate and destiny. No, never. Remember, if you leave your child on his fate and destiny, God will also leave you on your fate and destiny. God also knows tit-for-tat principle and India is a live example of it. So, if you love and care your children, God will also love and care you. In fact, God loves the children most. He sends them with a great hope that they will develop a healthy and beautiful humanity on earth. So we should all help God in fulfilling his pious and divine aim.

A Letter to the Young-Indians

Dear Young-Indians,

You are little-gems of India!

You are the real young Indians! I consider my child Vibhav—12 years old, a young-Indian. So, you all children are the real young-Indians and you are its future. In fact, it is only in your hand to make India rich, healthy, strong and prosperous—or keep it poor, populated, corrupt and polluted as it is now.

If you want to make future of India bright and beautiful, the first and foremost thing you need is—you must have to be educated; yes you must be educated. You must all get a minimum level of education. Even you are the poorest of the poor child of India; you must make effort to get a minimum level of education. What is the minimum level—10th or 10+2 standard. I consider that if a child gets this minimum-level of education and he understands and absorbs everything what is written in his school text books, he gets enough understanding to live a normal human life. He may not get a job, and seeing the present competition-level for job, it is sure that he will not get a job with this minimum level of education, but he will certainly get a minimum level of knowledge and understanding to live a healthy life, and that I want.

I want everyone to live sensibly as a human being and not like animals as we were living thousands of years back in jungle. In the olden days, if one person had become a Buddha or Mahavira, it does not mean that every person of that age was living like Buddha and Mahavira. If people of that age were living like Buddha and Mahavira, then to whom Buddha and Mahavira were teaching—don't tell lie, don't steal, don't drink alcohol, don't quarrel, don't go to prostitution…etc.—why these teachings to saint people! So, in the beginning, we were animal and we are transforming and developing from animal to man; we are becoming monkey to man, and education plays the maximum role in making us man—a sensible human being.

Many people, and especially villagers, opine that if education cannot give job to our children, then what is the use and value of education. They argue that if our children, after education, will work in field like a labour then what is the value of education. Then it is better they start working in field earlier—in their very childhood. Because, after getting education, they hesitate to work in field—they think that they are now educated—graduates and post-graduates, and hence they feel shame working like a labour in field. At that time, they think to get a white-colour job and work in an office. They do not want to make dirty their hands. Logic of such people is also somewhat right and practical, but this way of thinking is an animal-way-thinking—just do work and eat and sleep like an ass, that's all.

Life is only for eating and sleeping and nothing else. Really, situation is very critical and to make understand these people is a tough task. Due to ignorance, they are not ready to accept our logic and suggestions. They easily discard our logic and suggestions. I have a simple solution for it—control population of India, reduce it below 75 crores. For this, give birth to only one child, or be childless if you are extremely poor—in the next birth, means after 50-60 years, we will all certainly get a job with sufficient salary to enjoy a good life—educated or uneducated—we will all get a labour or a clerk job with a justified salary. Otherwise, we will all have sufficient lands (at least 10 to 15 *bigha* per family with 1 or 2 children) for agriculture to earn enough income to live happily. If we cannot do this, sorry, we all can never live happily—never means never. If you want to confirm this matter with prime-minister or president of India, you can confirm it. And if you know God, you can also confirm it with God! I am saying this because I have already confirmed it with God! Only crying and blaming government and leaders is not going to solve poverty and unemployment problem. You cry or die—who cares, no one. Leaders are only for doing survey, discussion, planning and delivering speech—especially when election comes; they have no time to care you. In fact, ground reality is that, even your parents and family members do not care you properly—what to say government and leaders.

I was also in the same position while struggling for getting a job. Even my family and my father had left me to struggle on my own caliber. My father had once told me in a totally angry-mood—you do whatever you want to do, I have no money for you, and I don't care what you are doing! And after this incidence, I felt so embarrassed and disgusted that I had totally stopped asking money from him. I had started taking tuition of children for money. I have self-respect. I cannot ask like a beggar from my parents. You know, I never pray even God like a beggar. I consider God as my friend and not my boss. So, I talk God as my friend, I share my difficulties as well as my happiness with him in a friendly manner.

However, I have no complaint with my mother. She had loved and cared me a lot. But friends, only love and care is not enough, we need money—not in lakhs and crores but at least in hundreds and thousands, only then a poor young can struggle and compete with others. And therefore, I say, if you have no money for caring your child—do not give birth to him. This message I want to give to the whole India—and especially to the youths of India, as they are going to give birth to their children.

Friends, we should understand that we do not get education only for getting a job. No, in fact we get education to become a human being in a true manner. Without education, our thinking will be childish, outdated and obsolete. We cannot think in a logical and scientific manner. If I am writing this book, I am writing it because I have read a lot. Reading has made me more sensible and awakened. It has sharpened my thinking. Today, I can talk even God with my thinking, reasoning and awareness! I will not stand in front of God simply praying and praising him, saying I love you and requesting him to take me to your abode, because I do not want to live in this corrupt and painful world. Instead of saying all these nonsense, I will discuss him the human and social issues as I am discussing them in this book.

Understand that I have not read only for getting better degrees and better jobs, but I have read to be more sensible and awakened. Even I had got a fire officer-training from a reputed college (NFSC Nagpur), after getting an ordinary but stable and secured job in Indian Navy, I had stopped running behind a better job and better salary. Though my father and friends had advised me to attempt for a better job, but I did not do that.

I have no interest in running life-long behind jobs just to earn more money. I can never do that. In fact, if I had a great interest to earn lots of money as I had a great desire to eradicate my poverty (I was ready to fight even God for this, if He has written poverty in my fate and destiny), I would have become a rich man very early in my life! How! I had gone for a bank robbery! Yes, I want to hit my target in a straight way; why to go in politics or do other business to earn more money? Just hit the target straight and everyone knows that no risk no gain and more risk more gain! So, my view is very straight and clear. What I want wholeheartedly, I put my total efforts for that—pass or fail; I don't care. I want to eradicate poverty and unemployment completely from India and world, and therefore I am putting my total efforts for it.

I remember, once a professor had told me when I was in 10+2, "Self-study is the best-study" and I found that he was absolutely correct. While teaching my child, I usually quote the same quotation to him. Following the same quote, I have studied nearly all important and valuable books written on human and social development from the age of Vedas to the age of modern science—spirituality, religion, philosophy, psychology, social-science, humanity, self-help, motivational, modern science…every filed. I have not left any field. I want to absorb everything from every field. From the age of 15 (10th standard), I have been studying these books and still I have continued it.

In 3000 years, many great people have been born on this planet and they have all shared their valuable ideas, experiences and awareness. So only by studying them we can understand their views and experiences. Just by hanging their pictures on wall and praying them, we cannot understand them! And I strongly feel to say the same thing to you—every child.

In fact, I do not like to speak to the aged people, as they do not listen to me. They are already filled with so many myths and beliefs that they simply reject my logic—saying that I am a child now! They say, when I will be aged and old, I can understand them and their myths and beliefs in a better way. And therefore, I want to speak to only children and youth. I am sure you will understand me better. And friends, suppose, I am wrong at any point, you can correct me; you can frankly share your views with me. I am writing this book as a friend and not as a teacher or a guru. So you can correct me at any point. I just want to create a strong thinking in young people of India—that we can change and develop India. Yes, it is possible and we have to make it possible. We just need a little understanding and sensibility and we can change India.

Therefore, I strongly feel to say every child of India that, with education, you will get a job or not—don't bother. You need education to become a human being and not to get a job. If you think that you are a human being and not an animal, you must be educated. Without education, a human being is like an animal. There is no much difference between an uneducated human being and an animal. So, you must educate yourself up to a minimum level—at least up to 10+2 level. Your parents may not be educated and they may not be interested in sending you to school, but you must take deep interest in studies.

After being minimum educated, you do whatever you want to do—you work as a farmer, or sell vegetables, or open a kiraanaa shop, or work in a factory… or whatever you like to do for your survival. If I had not got a job, I myself had been doing one of these jobs (but frankly speaking, I do not want to imagine my life as a poor and unemployed. That imagination is very painful for me.) So, in your life, you do whatever you want to do, but you must be educated.

More importantly, for your illiteracy, do not blame your poverty and your parents. No, you need a strong desire, a passion for studies—that level of passion, which has been shown in a movie—'I am Kalam', only then you can become another Kalam, you will be highly educated and a high-level of sensible and intelligent person. So, let parents be illiterate and poor (they will be educated in their next birth!) but you—the young Indian must be educated. If you want to change India you must be educated and sensible.

Further, to be educated, do not depend only on your school and teachers. No, you create an intense-desire within you to be educated and make effort for it. For this, try yourself to understand whatever is written in your text-books. Always keep in mind that self-study is the best study. I myself have been educated in the same way.

I have mostly self-studied. You can easily understand the position of a government school of a village in Bihar and you can imagine their position 25 years back. Just 4 years back my village has got electricity and still it has to get a concrete road. So, you can imagine the position of my village 25 years back. Hence, I myself had made effort to understand every subject to my level best. Of course, school teachers had also helped me, and still, I had not forgotten my class-teacher Sri Bharat Master, who had lighted my inner-spark with his caring and sudden-love! (I have mentioned detailed story later.) Therefore, the first and foremost important thing is that you need an intense-desire to know and understand a subject and naturally you will start understanding the subject. You have power and intelligence, but until you create an intense-desire within you—your inner-power cannot work. Our soul needs an intense desire to work its best. So, be educated and change India with your great work and intelligence.

Remember, just wanting of anything is not enough (like Mr. Chetan Bhagat has written—What Young India Wants). Instead of wanting a thing, we need to make effort to fulfill our wants. Everyone wants a good life—white-colour job, money, power, property, status, fun and entertainment; but how many of us have got these things—few, very few.

Therefore, I say, from food-to-God (*bhojan se lekar bhagwan tak*) whatever you want, make effort for that. Without making efforts, you are not going to get anything. And, if you get a thing by luck or chance, or by-birth—because, many rich and millionaires have become rich in the same manner; you will lose that thing in the same manner, that is, by luck or chance, or through re-birth. If you can become a born-millionaire, then you can also become a born-slumdog. Therefore, if you want to get anything forever, get it by your own work and effort—this is the only way to get a thing forever.

Thank you very much for reading this long letter! I know you have no time and patience to read such a long letter, so I am thankful to you for your patience. Finally, I will be happy hearing something from you. My contact details are mentioned at "To the Reader" page of the book. You can share your problems and difficulties with me and I assure you that I will help you to my best of knowledge and experience. All the best and God bless you!

Truly yours,

Abhay, a Young-Indian!

An Incidence That Changed My Student-Life:

In my childhood, I had difficulty in memorizing data and information. I was a slow-learner. I had been mostly promoted from lower to higher classes up to 5th standard. In 5th standard, an incidence had been occurred in such a way that it had changed my student life. This incident had created a small-spark in my slow-learning student life. It had enhanced my interest in studies many times more. I want to describe this incidence, especially for slow-learner students.

At that time, I was studying at my village's school (KK High School, Sanjhouli, Rohtas, Bihar). Once it happened that my class teacher Sri Bharat Master had given homework in mathematics to memorize some definitions of numbers. Next day, just in very beginning of the class, he had started asking definitions of numbers and had punished whoever had not memorized the definitions. In punishment, he was rashly beating with a bamboo stick. Really, in olden days, classes were very dangerous! I remember clearly, he had beaten every student—not a single student was left, and after punishing nearly 30 students he had reached to me. You can imagine my position!

Although, I was a stupid student, I had tried my best to memorize definitions of some numbers at home and I had been succeeded in memorizing a single definition, and that was the simplest one "*ginati kee sankhyaa ko praakritic sankhyaa kahate hain*"(counting numbers are called natural numbers). So I collected my total-courage and I murmured this definition as a dying-soul, and I had just saved! You can imagine my position! How much relief I was feeling at that moment! He had also asked me some other definitions and I had tried to say something but what; I could not remember today. After me, a few students were left to be asked, but sorry to say, all were punished.

Out of nearly 50 students, only I was saved. One of the most foolish students of the class was saved! All the students were looking at me with a strange-look. How it became possible—all were thinking and discussing. I was also feeling very strange within me—thrilled and motivated. Slowly a voice was arising within me—"I can read, yes, I can read; I am not a stupid child."

After this incidence, I had been slowly progressed in my studies, and at the end of 5th class, I was counted in brilliant students of the class. Really, Sri Bharat Master had stimulated my soul unknowingly. Just by giving value to my little-effort and sincerity, he had lighted my inner-spark, my soul. He had made me a hero of the class for a day. Though, he had not done anything especial for me from his side, yet I know that he is the first teacher who had sparked my soul. Surely, my fire was within me—I had got it by-birth, but it was he who had first given a small-spark to my fire. He had unknowingly lighted that fire and and hence I will be ever grateful to him.

I hope, from this simple but real incidence of my real life, slow-learning students as well as teachers and parents will learn a good lesson. We must give value to little effort of our children. In one day, we cannot make them a doctor or an engineer. No, no one can do it. Even God is included in this no one list! God is not a magician. If God has produced some Einsteins, then He has also produced many idiots!

In fact, in this world, idiots are many times more (approx 10 times) than a few Einsteins. So, we should give value to little effort of a child—don't make him Einstein in one day and you know the position of Albert Einstein in his childhood. He was a stupid child. So, think how you can light a little-spark in your child and always make effort for it. Through my writing, I am also making an effort to give a small-spark in all the souls of India—especially to the souls of children and youths to change and develop India. We have to change India at any cost—take it as our vision and mission. We have reached our boiling-point for change and India is going to change very soon. We are going to prove Nostradamus prediction true that India will again become a 'Super-power' in the world. Although, I do not believe in such predictions, I strongly feel that India has reached its boiling-point for change and hence India is going to change and develop very soon.

Love Proved Stronger Than Bamboo-Stick!: Before punishing your child, think for a while about your own childhood and your childish behaviours at that time. Here, I recall a very bad incident happened in my childhood. As I was a slow-learner student and I had no interest in studies, I was mostly interested in playing or wandering here and there in my village. One day, it so happened that in the evening I had returned home very late and for this reason, my uncle-grandfather had cruelly beaten me. Really, this incident was very disgusting and cruel and even today if I remember it; I become very scared and emotional. My uncle-grandfather had beaten me nearly 15-20 times with a hard bamboo-stick! Imagine that cruelty! My whole body was painted with red lines! He was beating me even more and more because I was not crying and weeping; I was not begging pardon and requesting him to stop. I was just standing silent bearing the pain. Not a single cry and not a single drop in my eyes!

After cruelly-beaten, I had gone to home. My mother was making chapattis. Looking at me, my mother had just asked me—*kya hua mere lal!* (What happened my lovely son?) And I had started weeping bitterly. Now it had become difficult for me to stop my tears, (even at this moment I have tears in my eyes…). What a strong-body (my uncle-grandfather was a *pahalwaan*—body-builder of olden days) and a hard bamboo-stick had been proved failure to do, just a few words of my loving mother had done it. Who is stronger—think yourself!

Children Need a Feel-Free-to-Ask Type Class—and Not Just Feeding of Data: In the name of education, what we usually do—we simply feed data and information into young minds considering them a computer; and children learn those data as parrots learn. Students keep those data in their brains—with a great difficulty (I had also this difficulty and still I have it), without absorbing the essence and the context of those data. With a great difficulty, they try to remember those data and for this, they make many revisions day and night. But, they do not think creatively about what-why and how of those data. In fact, we have given so much burden of syllabus on them that they have no time to think innovatively about those data. Their teachers also do not motivate them for the same—which is their first duty. The teachers do not give them thinking and imagination to see our society and humanity with a broad view.

I consider that to develop self-thinking of students and to make them innovative and creative, we need an interactive and a feel-free-to-ask type class. Let our students free to think, ask, imagine, dream, analyse, and judge in their own ways. Surely, we will guide them but with our logic, reasoning, intelligence and awareness and not by huge burden of syllabus, complaints and scolding, and pressure and punishment. No, this is not the right way. Right way is—interaction, discussion, experiments and feel-free-to-ask type class. Only then, we can develop our children in a true manner, and later, these children—the gems of India, will develop a healthy, strong and a developed India.

"God Is Only One but He Is Everywhere, How?" One Day My Son Asked Me: Daily, at evening, I spend at least two hours with my son (if I am not seriously writing)—for playing, especially cricket, and for teaching-cum-self-study with him. I request all parents to spend a few hours daily with their children—you play or teach-cum-self-study with him, or in whatever way you like to interact with him. This is very effective in their healthy growth and development. Some parents complain that they have no time for their children. To these parents and all newly married couple, I would like to say that if you have no time for your kids, please do not give birth to them! Just enjoy your life. In fact, my child has been also taken birth quickly (in very first year of my marriage) only because of my wife's great desire. After marriage, my wife has done this job on an urgent basis, why, I do not know!

Anyway, once it happened that my child (at that time, he was 9 years old) was studying his moral-values book and while studying, at a sudden, he asked me, "Where is God?" I replied, "I don't know." He asked me again, "It is written in the book that God is only one but he is everywhere—how is it possible?" I was impressed with his reasoning. I replied, "Yes, you are right. It is not possible. It can be possible only when God will be many. Otherwise, if we suppose this universe (existence) as God then it can be possible, because this universe is only one but it is everywhere. Otherwise, it is never possible that a thing will be only one and it will be available everywhere in the universe."

Here, I would like to mention that my son has also a keen interest in science and universe. He wants to know more and more about planets, solar system, stars, and galaxy. In fact, he wants to become an astronaut and a cricketer as well! He may be the first cricketer who will play cricket on the moon! So, he easily understood what I wanted to convey him. Apart from this, I told him that it is not necessary to assume this universe as God, because this universe is universe—why to assume it as God; no, there is no need. So, if you don't want to consider this universe as God and you think that God is something else, because your thinking may be different from mine, then in my view, first you try to know about nature and universe and then about God. God is not first but the last thing to know! First, you know about everything and then you try to know about God.

People generally do this mistake, without knowing the basic things; they directly want to know about God. People are in hurry to do and to get everything quickly, but they do not know that even top-level scientists like Einstein and Newton could not understand God completely. So, in my view, first be intelligent and capable to take a Noble prize (also,India needs Noble prizes as India has very few Noble prizes!) and then you hope that you can understand God a little.

To know God, we have to understand everything—from atom to black-hole; and in India, the understanding-level of common-people is so poor that they do not know even a-b-c-d about atom, what to say about black-hole, which is like our God—invisible and most powerful! Even light cannot fly around a black-hole, what to say a bird! And this is not the situation of only less-educated people like 10th pass, but this is the situation of many graduates and post-graduates.

For these people, education means only job and a better salary, that's all (*naukari and chhokari*—as writer Mr. Chetan Bhagat says). Their education is finished when they think that they cannot get a better job than what they have. What is an atom, atom knows. They don't bother to know about an atom! They don't bother to know about relation between time and space. It is the work of a scientist like Einstein and not theirs.

Therefore I say to my child, first you know and experience whatever you study through your books and through your teachers and me—and especially through your own-self—

through your own mind, feelings and experiences, and then you try to know about God. Always remember, God is not first but the last thing to know. Even you would be able to know a little about God at the last moment of your life; it will be a great rather the greatest thing of your life. So, do not be in a hurry to know about God. Be slow, have patience and think with a calm and relaxed mind.

As a matter of fact, I myself talk a lot of things about God, but I know about myself that I know very little about God—very little. However, I am such a man who, only on the basis of this little knowledge, can talk any world-guru or universe-guru about God!

Thus, about God, I did not give my child any false and outdated myths and beliefs; instead, I just put my views in front of him in a friendly manner. And, I consider that this is the correct way of teaching and awakening others; and through this book, I have made effort for the same. I observe that due to lack of simple reasoning and understanding, people are living a miserable and stressful life, and until their reasoning and conscience are developed, their misery and stress can never be ended. No leader, guru, god or government can end their problems, it 100% sure.

Moreover, here, we should understand that only with such an interaction with our children, we can develop them with a healthy-mind and awakening-soul, and only this can develop a healthy society and humanity where there will be no differences and quarrellings due to different belief-systems about God. In fact, I am such a man who says, if we have quarrel and war due to different Gods and religions then we should leave all Gods and religions! Let die all Gods and religions! Also, the body which I consider as God is a totally different one. I consider nature and existence as God and we know that this God always loves and cares us. So, only because of our ignorance and misunderstanding about our religions, gurus and god-men, we quarrel and fight among ourselves. This quarrel and fight can be stopped only with developing our awareness and conscience.

We Are Not Computers, We are Creator of Computer!: As I have mentioned earlier that in case of students and children, we consider a human brain as a computer and we feed data in to them as we do in a computer. Computer helps us in thinking-and-making plan and hence we think that computer is like a human body. However, there is a big difference between a computer and a human body, and that difference is because of our inbuilt conscience and awareness—our soul. In fact, in modern science age, I should not use the word soul frequently here and there in my writings—as modern and advance people do not believe in soul. But I am using this term repeatedly because I want that modern science investigates into this matter on an urgent basis.

I want that modern science should prove that what people like Sri Krishna and Gautama Buddha had told thousands of years back, is true and genuine. Science must prove that such people are not phony and fake but they are genuine and trustworthy people. We modern and advance people may be fake, selfish, opportunists and corrupt, but such olden-and-golden people are not fake and phony. They are sincere and trustworthy people and I want to confirm their sincerity and truthfulness through modern science.

So, we have a soul, an inbuilt and nature-made mechanism, which makes us different from a computer. Like every natural body—like an atom or a cell, we have an inbuilt-nucleus which controls and guides our whole mechanism. Whereas, being an artificial body, a computer has not such an inbuilt mechanism—and never it can have (we may make movie like Robot—staring superstar Rajanikanth—really it is an entertaining movie), and therefore, a computer can never control and guide its inner-mechanism itself. For every little action, it will need our command. In fact, this is the reason why even the most stupid person of the world can do so many things without any teaching and learning; but a computer can do nothing without programming it. For every little action, a computer needs a coded-command. Without programming, it is just an iron-box; and even it is programmed, without electricity it is an iron-box!

Besides, we should understand that we can only create and develop new version of programming (or software) for a computer but we can never create 'soul' in a computer. What existence has created in billions of years, we cannot create them in a month or a year. Science may try for it, but in my experience and awareness, science can never succeed in it.

In fact, as per my understanding, science should think and make effort for solving problems like poverty, unemployment, illiteracy, population-explosion, pollution, global-warming etc. Scientists should not waste their valuable time in experimenting on small issues like human-cloning, artificial-intelligence etc. I consider scientists as the real leaders of world and humanity, and they must prove it by leading and saving this world and humanity. I do want to say every child that if you become a scientist, think and make effort to save earth and humanity—this should be your first and foremost job.

So, a computer can never work like a human being. Surely, it can think, calculate and work many times faster than a human being, but it can never work like us. It can never think and imagine like us. It can never feel and experience like us. Most importantly, it can never work by itself—means, a soul can never be created in a computer or in a robot. Therefore, though a computer can work millions times faster than a human-mind, it can never be equal to a human being. Our soul—our thinking, imagination, awareness, creativity, feelings and emotions, makes the greatest difference between a man and a computer. Therefore, remember, we are creator of computers and we will be always controller of them.

We Are Just Care-Taker and Not Creator of Our Children: Why it happens that the children of the same parents show a noticeable dissimilarity among one another? Why even twins born of the same parents and brought up under similar environments show dissimilarity in between them? How theory of heredity-transmission and genetic engineering can explain this case? And, how astrology—which says that the position of stars and planets affect the fate and destiny of a child—can explain 'twin-birth' case; because twins are born at the same time and at the same place? So this question naturally rises that who or what is creating this dissimilarity? Who is playing a diplomatic or political game with our children as well as with our reproductive system! And, please stop saying—God knows!

In fact, we instantly bring God whenever we find difficulty in explaining such a case. This mentality shows our poor reasoning and awareness. So, first we should use our reasoning and logical power and then we should involve God in our discussion. Secondly, we should involve God from a scientific perspective and not from an old and obsolete religious-and-spiritual perspective.

Science and scientists also speak about God, but they talk with a reasoning and sensibility. They do not simply declare anything like a guru or god-man. Besides, today even spiritual experiences like existence of soul and life-after-death can be checked with the help of devices of modern science. In fact, modern science has seen soul but till now, it has not the complete picture about it. There are many how-and-whys about soul which need to be checked and clarified and science is investigating into this matter.

Modern science says that heredity plays an important role in transmission of our virtue and talent in our children. But I am not agreed with it. I consider that heredity plays a role only in making physical part of our child—length, breath, height, size, colour etc. It does not play any role in transferring our art and virtue into our children. Otherwise, every doctor-couple should produce doctor-children and every engineer-couple should produce only engineer-children. But it does not happen so in real life.

My son wants to be a cricketer (but with growing, slowly he is changing his mind and I do not know why?), but I have never dreamed to become a cricketer. Surely, I have interest to play cricket and I play it. I also watch cricket match—especially last two overs of a 20-20 live-cricket match, but my son watches even a 20 years old test-cricket match! Such a stupid fellow he is! Besides, from 6th standard, I have been watching a change in him—he is being addicted of cartoon-channels. One day, when I had asked him why you have been addicted of cartoons—do you want to become a cartoon! He answered—Yes, I want to be a cartoon!

Young-India is like this! Whatever they like—they do—right or wrong—they don't care! I like it and I do it, that's all—this is their reply. But we, the adult-India, the matured India, have to care our young-India. We cannot simply leave them to spoil and become a cartoon! If India has been spoiled and become a cartoon now, it is only because we have not properly cared our young-India. We need to correct our mistake, only then we can transform cartoon-India into a developed country.

I do not know what my son would become, but I will be happy if he would become a teacher or a professor. In fact, when I had been failed to pass engineering entrance test with a good scoring, I had decided to become a teacher, but again I could not succeeded. What a fate! I neither become a scientist nor a teacher; I become a fire-fighter and a storekeeper, about which I had never thought! Really, if I would think from a luck and fate point of view then my luck and fate are really bad; but I never think in that way. I am such a person who—even God comes in front of me in a human form (as people think), and tell me to believe in fate and destiny—I cannot accept his fate and destiny concept. I will put up my views in front of him, as I have put them in my writings. I argue him and if I could not convince him, I would say, I am agreed to disagree with you! Yes, I am agreed to disagree with God! I would say to God, you keep your views and your fate and destiny concept with you, I do not need them.

So, when I could not become what I had decided and dreamed about myself, how I can decide about my son—no, I cannot. So, I just help him in his becoming—his flowering and blooming, his growing and developing. I am just a care-taker of my child and not his master and creator. I usually say to him—first you should be educated to a minimum level, and at least, you should study to become a clerk, as without a minimum level education, a common man cannot get a clerk job.

Also, in this age of competitions (only because of high population), becoming even a clerk is not an easy task. Many graduates and post-graduates are trying hard to get a clerk-grade job but they are not getting it. Hence, I say to him, first you should be educated to become a clerk and then you become a cricketer or whatever you want—it will be your wish and decision—I least bother about that. Here, I would also like to thank KBC and Mr. Amitabh Bachchan, because through this show my son came to know that cricketer MS Dhoni, who is his role-model, has started his carrier as a TTE, a clerk-grade job. So, it will work as a great inspiration for my son and every youngster.

Therefore, we should understand that the actual creator of our children is nature and existence (the real God) and not we. We can only help them in their development but we cannot shape them as per our dream and planning. We can also understand this matter with this simple analogy: a soul is like a seed of a plant. Its virtue and potential are coiled up within its core as it happens in case of a seed. After taking birth, a soul slowly starts growing and emerging its virtue and potential. For seedling and growth of a child, a couple provides just a piece of land. Rich couples provide a fertile-land and poor couples provide a barren-land!

Again, as a seed, during its growth, receives and assimilates certain peculiarities from its environment—land, water, air etc.; similarly, a soul receives and assimilates some peculiarities like belief, habits, behaviour, culture etc. from his environment—parents, family, friends, teachers, school, society etc. However, the most important point to be aware of is that—while growth of a child, his soul or inner-potential plays the main role in his growth and development. It is basically his soul which coordinates and directs his thought-process, desires and actions—which are the key ingredients of development of a human being.

As we know, Albert Einstein was a silly boy in his early age. He was so silly that one of his teachers had declared that he could never study. Such a silly boy, one day, had become one of the greatest scientists of the world. It looks strange but it is reality. In fact, this is not only a single case; rather similar incidents have been happened in the lives of many intelligent and virtuous people of the world. So, here, the question rises that why such strange things happens in lives of some people? The answer is: it happens because such human beings have already acquired crystallization and awakening of their soul and therefore they have already developed their inbuilt virtue and intelligence.

When such an awakened and intelligent soul takes a new birth, his soul slowly starts opening its layers like the petals of a lotus where there is coiled-up sharp understanding and intelligence in a potential form. But we simply say that such people are special and God-gifted. Everyone cannot be like them. But this is a stupid logic. It is not the actual reality. Reality is that we are all God-gifted with some virtue and talent. Even an atom which is so tiny in size has been gifted with some virtue, so we—a huge molecule, have been gifted trillions times more than an atom. (I have explained clearly how a human body is like a molecule in my book 'How to Develop One & All'. Please read it at my website.) So, we just need to make effort to recognize and emerge our inbuilt virtue. Without self-effort, even God cannot do anything for us, what to say about a leader, guru or a god-man.

From the above discussions, it is clear that we are not master and creator of our children; but we are just their care-takers. Secondly, we do not need to create or insert art and virtue in our children; instead we just need to help them in emerging their inbuilt virtue. And though, it seems a very simple task, it is not so simple—because, a child is like a seed, a potential-unit, an unknown-chemistry and we have to reveal this chemistry. And certainly, to reveal this chemistry we need a certain level of education, awareness and a sense of responsibility towards development of our children. We need a careful observation, a friendly-interaction and a supporting behavior with them. Without this, we cannot develop our children in a proper manner and we cannot develop a healthy and developed India.

Make Dream for Oneself and Not For Your Child: From childhood to youth (until I got a government job), I had a joint-family and in my whole of joint-family, only my mother and my own grandfather were very loving and caring to me. However, my grandfather had made a big dream for me. He had dreamed to make me an IAS officer or at least an engineer, but as you know, I could not fulfill his dream. I should be sorry for that but I am not, because my idea is—make dream for oneself and not for others. If you make dream for other and you force him to fulfill it then you create trouble for both yourself and for other too.

Becoming an IAS officer, an engineer, a doctor, or doing something great and wonderful…, these are dreams of every child. No one takes birth to do bad and evil things. Everyone is born with a dream, a spark—little or large, it does not matter, and everyone makes effort for it, but only a few get success. Success means—who get remarkable power, money, status, name and fame etc. What we should do—should we kill our other children if they prove failure in becoming what they have dreamed for themselves, or we have dreamed for them? I am saying this because some people are killing their children.

Though, these people will not be agreed with my saying, and reversely, they will argue that whatever they do, they do for making their children's future and carrier. But one day, suddenly something goes wrong—and parents are surprised—awkward; what happened and why it happened!? But sorry, it is too late, nothing can be done now; you have lost your child!? Now, you sit and cry, and rub your hands life-long! Therefore, child-caring, and especially in their teenage, is not a simple task. It needs lots of care and attention.

I had also made efforts to my level best to pass engineering competitions with a good scoring, but I could not make it. I had gone through a frustrating situation at that period of time. However, that time-period has gone, it is dead now. Now I am—what I am, and I am enjoying what I am—and that is the main thing in our life.

I know many children and especially youths are going through a frustrating situation as I have gone, and hence I do want to say them that whatever may be the situation—you face it. You kill the problem but never kill yourself—never commit suicide. If parents say—leave them—you leave them and face the world with your own capability and stamina; but never commit suicide. We are born here to live as per our own wish and desire and we should leave in the same way. We are not slaves or servants of our parents and family. We are not servants of even God. God is our friend and not boss.

Also, I request all parents and guardians that you help and support your child with your love and care. If you have given birth to them to live, grow and develop, then the first and foremost thing they need is—your love, care and support. Let them become what they think and believe, and what they want. Have some patience. And, if you are feared that your child will be spoiled if you will not scold him, guide him, and give pressure; then overcome your fear. There is a God who guides everyone—don't you feel so? If not—you need soul-treatment! Yes, you need inner-search—inner-peace, inner-awakening. You need yoga and meditation. Saying about yoga and meditation, you may think I am joking with you, but I do say that if you don't feel your inner-peace and don't listen to your inner-voice, then you are making joke with your life—you are spoiling your life. Be awake and stop spoiling your life and also life of your children.

You Are the Most Responsible For What You Are: In my young age, to motivate me towards studies, my grandfather used to tell me that children of only poor families become interested in studies. Children of rich families do not take interest in studies. They waste their parent's money in movies, fun and entertainment, gambling, girls, alcohol etc. I knew, saying this, he wanted to motivate me for doing hard work in studies and become an IAS officer. However, one day, being irritated listening to his usual stories, I had argued him in a different mood. I had asked him—why children of only poor families should study? He answered, to stand on their own feet—to get a job, to earn money, to be rich and prosperous. I argued—but when a poor would get a job and he would become rich and prosperous—how his children would study, because now his children would become children of a rich parents. Now his children would waste money in movies, fun and entertainment, gambling, girls, alcohol etc.—as you say. Therefore, it is better a poor child should never study so that his children would always study. Otherwise, after studies, if a poor child gets a chance to get a job and earn money, he should not earn money. He should always remain poor so that his money could not spoil his children. Hearing my logic my grandfather had no reply!

Friends, no one studies due to his poverty or prosperity and no one spoils due to money, wealth and prosperity. A person studies or does good things in his life and move forward only because of his inner-awareness and inner-virtue and nothing else. Reversely, a person spoils his life due to poor intensity of his inner-awareness—his weak soul. Besides, if a weak-soul gets birth in a family of weak-souls, the speed of his spoiling increased many folds—in Hindi, it is said—*din dunaa aur raat chougunaa*, means, in day two times and at night four times! However, in reverse, if he gets parents, family and society of strong and enlightened souls, these people try their level best to strengthen and develop him. They share their knowledge, experience and intelligence with him and motivate him to think in an intelligent way.

Therefore, only a child is not fully responsible for his underdevelopment and spoiling, but his parents, family and society are also 'somewhat' responsible. I am saying somewhat, because a soul which has been taking birth from so many lives—sometimes among rich and prosperous, and sometimes among poor and downtrodden. So during this birth-rebirth process, he sees so many human-flowers in humanity—people like Sri Krishna, Gautama Buddha, Kabir, Nanak etc.; people like Plato, Socrates, Karl Marks etc.; and people like Galileo, Copernicus, Edison, Newton, Einstein etc. are human-flowers. Now seeing these human-flowers if he does not inhale and absorb the virtue and fragrance of these human-flowers, then who is responsible for his negligence and weakness—only he himself and no one else? So, obviously he himself is the most responsible for his negligence, ignorance and poor development.

He may blame God, guru, religion, society, government, parents, family, nation, leaders, fate, destiny, planets, stars etc…etc. But frankly speaking, these are all just excuses—man-made excuses. Reality is that a person himself is the most responsible for his underdevelopment, poverty and poorness. And this is the reason, sometimes I think—let happen whatever is happening; let die the dying and rot be rotting! You know I had left even my mother to die! After a quarreling in my joint-family, she was trying to consume poison and at the very same moment I had entered home from outside. But even after seeing her committing suicide, I did not throw poison-bottle from her hand. I was just two steps away from her, but I did not catch her hand. There were tears in my eyes and my hands had been folded into fists but I did not move a single step to save her—I left her to decide herself what she wanted to do—if she wanted to die let her die. How many times I can save you, how many times I will be in front of you—so, you live or die in your own interest; you take decision in your own interest. However, my mother is still alive because, at that moment, when she had looked at me she had kept the poison-bottle. And this incident had been occurred only because of poverty and indirectly because of unemployment of my father.

At present, if poor people of India have been reached in a miserable and dying situation, it is only because, people are unable to understand the criticality of situation. They are not ready and capable to take their responsibility. They simply hope from government and pray to guru and God that one day their problems may be solved. And I say, until you leave hope from government, guru and God, and you think yourself in an intelligent manner; your problems can never be solved. You yourself have to think and act to solve your problems. Government, guru, God etc. may help you but a little—very little, because we poor are in billions and Government, guru and God have not sufficient resources to help us. So we have to control population and we should also think and act to solve our problems on our own level.

If we think in other way, for a human being—poverty, sorrow, pain, misery etc. are also good things to experience! When you take birth in a rich family—have fun, enjoyment and entertainment; and reversely, when you take birth in a poor family—cry, weep, blame, rot and die or commit suicide. Doing these exercises, ultimately one day your soul will start awakening—it will start seedling and sprouting. So, God changes our plot, our level, and our ground to make us sprout and grow in a perfect manner. God moves us in different energy levels to show our potential, stamina and capability; as it moves electrons of an atom in different energy levels to make strong chemical bonds with other atoms and to give better products. Hence, poverty, sorrow, misery, and rotting of lives are not as bad as we see them in some movies like Slumdog-millionaire or as we read in some real or fictional stories. They are good for our seedling and sprouting and ultimately awakening. I have also a good experience of these things in this life; however I am not in a position to experience them again! And therefore, I want to eradicate total poverty and unemployment from India and world.

Therefore friends, understand that you are the most responsible for what you are today. Of course, my mother is also responsible for what she is today, and I say the same thing to her. I do not say only goody-goody things to her or to my any other relatives. I talk them in the same manner as I talk to you in this book. Therefore, you do not think that you are a lucky or unlucky fellow. God does not make anyone lucky or unlucky. In fact, God has no idea about luck and fate. Connecting success, money, power, status etc. with our luck, fate, destiny, lines of hands and head, position of stars and planets etc.—these are only our way of thinking and dreaming. We ourselves have created these thinking, beliefs and stories. God has no concern with these beliefs and stories. So, God may change your plot, your story-line at any moment—be prepared to face the challenges. Take care! ✌

7

Healthy Way of Life

Baba Ramdev—A Real Mover-and-Shaker of India!

It is bad to hear but it is a hard-truth that India is a lazy country! Most of Indians are lazy and dull. They want everything readymade and easily served. Food, shelter, money, health, security, knowledge, information, God… everything should be readily available. They want only roses of life but not its thrones. They do not want to take risk in life—everything should go in a smooth way as it is going—no change. This poor thinking-and-attitude has made us lazy and dull.

At this stage, we need a person like Baba Ramdev, who can move and shake our body and mind. He is a real Mover-and-Shaker of India. (Mr. Shekhar Suman is a filmy Mover-and-Shaker and at present, Mr . Kapil Sharma is doing the same job through his TV show Comedy Night with Kapil. Really it is an entertaining show and it is also one of my favorite TV shows. Mr Kapil Sharma seems me 'Modern Laughing-Buddha'! Just his smiling face is enough to make us laugh!)

Baba Ramdev does not only speak but also does what he says. He has done a great job to make Indians healthy and still he is doing his job with a great enthusiasm. In history of India, I do not see any such a man like him. I have great respect for this man. Though, I have little difficulty accepting his political views, as I want all leaders and political parties of India to work together for development of India. No Congress, no BJP, no Left, no

Right, no Third or Fourth-Front..., nothing. We all have to work together—not only leaders but also common men, only then we can change India.

I am going to send 25 copies of this book to the Parliament House of India for top-leaders of India so that they can read it and understand the situation in a better way. So, I have little difficulty with the political views of Baba Ramdev, otherwise, he is a fantastic human being. I love such people. Three years back, when he had come to Visakhapatnam, I had touched his feet and taken his blessings. I had also presented my books to him. In fact, wherever I find an opportunity to present my book to a leader, dignitary or a VIP, I do not miss it.

Yoga—A Scientific and Broad View: In my awareness and understanding, the word yoga (a Sanskrit word which means addition or connection), is a symbol to represent the connectivity, integrity and harmonious unity of all the units and systems of the existence. For a human being, yoga is an experience to feel this whole existence as a single-system. In this existence, there are many kinds of matters and materials—from huge black holes to the tiny atoms; and among all these big and small bodies there exists a harmonious relation.

Friends, ignore the differences of human world for a few moments and observe the harmonious unity of this universe—there is a harmonious unity among all the galaxies, among all the stars of a galaxy, and among all the planets and moons of a star. Our sun is also such a star and we observe this harmonious unity in our solar system too. This harmonious unity is nothing but yoga in a broad sense. So, what Albert Einstein tried to define through his modern concept of theory of relativity, the olden awakened and intelligent people have made effort to describe the same thing through yoga. Hence, in a broad sense, yoga represents the harmonious unity and integrity of every unit and system of the existence, which is our real God.

We Need Yoga-Attitude to Maintain Harmony on Earth: Observing the harmonious unity and integrity of nature and existence, we should be aware that there should be also a harmonious unity among all the matters and materials of our planet earth. In fact, in the past, there was a natural harmony on our mother earth. However, with the progress and advancement of human society, the natural harmony of earth was disturbed; and for this, we people are maximum responsible. We have nearly destroyed its harmony to fulfill our unlimited desires and dreams of power, money and status; and now we have arrived at an alarming stage—a now-or-never stage. Therefore, now it high time and it is our sole responsibility to maintain this harmony, and we should take strong steps in this direction as soon as possible.

However, it is matter of great shame that when the matter comes to maintain this harmony, we mostly play blame-game. We blame one another for the problems. But this blame-game is not going to solve our problems. Our problems will be solved only by understanding the actual cause of problems and helping and supporting one another. We need a yoga-attitude—we have to consider this earth as a joint-family and we have to help one another as family-members. More importantly, maintaining this harmony is the basic responsibility of all the leaders and the government-bodies of the world. It is a challenge for their intelligence, awareness and capability. And though, I am a common man, I felt a certain responsibility to do something in this regard, and therefore I expressed my views through this book; so that people may be aware of the actual reality and do something to rectify these problems.

Yoga and Meditation—A Healthy Way of Life: Common people think that yoga is some sorts of physical exercises like other physical exercises of our body; but this is not the actual reality. In fact, the real aim of yoga is to crystallize our inner-energy (soul) for creating a harmonious relation between our soul and the creator existence. The physical exercises of our body are just a little part of yoga. We may understand this matter in this way: as we know, everything of this universe is made-up of both mass and energy and our body is also made up of the same materials. Our body is nature-made and not man-made.

So, for the smooth functioning of mass (muscles and bones) of our body, we need physical exercises and for the smooth functioning of its energy we need meditation, that is, inner-peace. Thus, yoga has a great role in development of people, society and whole humanity; and since yoga has been started in India, India should be the first in development of its people and society. It should lead the whole world and prove that it is world-guru and not a world-*chella*. I am saying this because in present age, we are mostly following other countries. We have forgotten our olden-and-golden tradition, culture and heritage and blindly following others. We should stop this *chella*-culture.

The True Meaning of Meditation: For ages, we have read a lot of things about yoga and meditation. So I do not need to explain these things in details. However, here I want to discuss an important point about meditation. What is meditation in actual sense? In my experience and awareness, meditation is a very simple activity of our mind and soul. In fact, meditation is so simple that it looks absurd to mention it as an act or activity. Actually, I can describe meditation in only one sentence: meditation is nothing but simply-sitting and doing-nothing!

Generally, we always do something or think to do something (except in deep-sleep when we become no-mind!); however in meditation, we don't have to do even 'thinking'—so simple is meditation. We have to move neither our body nor our mind, and friend, do you know any activity simpler than this. No, there is no one and there can be never one. So, meditation is the simplest activity of a human being.

Now, why we need to do meditation and what is its value in development of a human being? In fact, meditation has a great value in our development. Meditation helps us in increasing our inner-peace and hence it helps us in crystallization of our inner-energy (soul)—which results into our inner-awakening and emergence of our art and virtue. As a matter of fact, only because of meditation and inner awakening, an illiterate person like Kabir Das had become an awakened and virtuous soul. He is a great surprise for India and the whole world. He is also a great inspiration for me as I am also an ordinary man like him. I often hear his virtuous-poetry and his poetry prove that he had a deep experience of life. So, Kabir Das is a great example of this fact that even an illiterate person with a crystallized-soul can be an awakened and virtuous human being. However, I am highly against illiteracy and we should understand that Kabir das was an illiterate because his parents were poor and illiterates; otherwise if he had been provided education, he had been a top-class intelligent person.

Further, though we think that we have developed to a modern science age, I observe that only a few people of this world (may be 10% or less), are able to sit in meditation for 5 to 10 minutes. Remaining 90% people, because of their poor crystallization of soul, cannot sit in meditation even for 5 minutes. They cannot sit in silence just for 5 minutes. Thinking is always going on in their minds. And such people are not only illiterate people but educated people too. In fact, the actual matter is that, education cannot make someone peaceful from within. Education gives us knowledge and information, it gives us thinking and mind, but it does not give us inner-peace and inner-awakening. We get inner-peace only by sitting or relaxing peacefully in our own interest. Therefore, for inner-peace, we should regularly sit or relax peacefully until we become capable to sit peacefully (no-thinking state) for 5 to 10 minutes.

One may ask that if meditation is so simple, why so many people are searching for spiritual gurus and gods to make them understand this matter. Friends, reality is that, behind every misunderstanding and ignorance, the reason is only one and that is poor-crystallization of one's soul, or say, poor self-awakening. Due to poor crystallization of soul, people have lack of awareness which results into misunderstanding and ignorance. Therefore, we have to crystallize our soul with the help of meditation, only then we can be peaceful, awakened and blissful.

Come out of All False Myths and Beliefs: From a long time back, we have been taught many dos and don'ts, shoulds and shouldn'ts by our ancestors and forefathers, and we have followed them without applying our own reasoning and sensibility. We have not questioned them; we have not argued them; we have simply followed them. Though, at present, we have come to the age of science and technology, still we believe in their sayings without asking why and how. Still we believe in luck, fate and destiny; in lines of hands and heads; and in position of planets and stars etc. Moreover, we have such a strong believe in our forefathers' beliefs that we are ready to face problems and difficulties but we are not ready to leave them. However, if we want to come out of our problems and difficulties, we must leave our false beliefs with our understanding and awareness.

In the age of science, we must think in a scientific and logical manner to understand the actual cause of a problem, only then we can solve our problems. Only our logical thinking and sincere-effort can solve our problems and nothing else. Therefore, it is the urgent need of time to come out of all false beliefs and work-out our total ability to develop a healthy India.

How Did We Trap In Belief-System?: It is very simple to understand: actually, the journey of mankind has been started with ignorance, difficulties and fear. Our minds have been conditioned with fear and ignorance from the ancient history. Just 5-6 thousand years back, on this earth, no one was a guru or god; no one was a king or queen, no one was a leader or genius—we were all more or less same. Actually science puts the real picture of our past. It clearly proves that in the past, we were all animals like other animals wandering here and there in jungles for our food and survival. Though, we believe that our ancestors were very clever and intelligent and we have been gradually become ignorant and corrupt; but it is not the actual reality.

Reality is that we have started our journey with difficulty, poverty, fear and ignorance and we have continuously progressed towards prosperity, fearlessness, awareness and intelligence, and today we have reached modern science age. So, because our journey of development has been started with fear, ignorance and difficulties, and hence we have been conditioned with false myths and beliefs. It was not our fault, in fact, it was not fault of anyone; it was a natural evolution process and it is still continued. However, with advancement of science and technology, we should come out of all false myths and beliefs and we should all make efforts for development of one-and-all.

Science Can Never Believe In Any Belief-System:

We should understand that science can never accept any belief or belief-system just because it has been told or created by a world famous guru or god-man. Science checks and verifies every matter to be fully sure about its reality. It doubts and hence it further investigates even the theories of world's top-level scientist like Albert Einstein and Isaac Newton. So how it can simply accept sayings of past gurus and god-men? No, it cannot accept. Actually, to believe and accept anything without knowing and experiencing its reality is ignorance and science is antonym of ignorance.

In fact, for science, not-knowing is many times far better than simply believing; because, if science will start believing, it can never progress. Doubt, search, investigation, experiment, and re-search—these are the basic tools of science without which science will be paralyzed and ultimately died, which is never possible. Science will always remain alive. And therefore, I say, science is the best teacher for everyone. Science always tries to speak about truth as honestly as possible. So, we should always rely on the findings of science and not on any belief-system. I myself consider science as my best teacher.

Drugs and Alcohol Cannot Solve Our Problems:

Tobacco, cigarette, alcohol and drugs have become big problems for our people and society. And not only educated but even illiterate people know that these materials are injurious to their health; even though they consume these harmful materials. What is the basic cause of their negligence towards their health and life, and their family too? I think we all know the answer—the answer is our day to day life's tension, stress, disappointment and depression. People drink alcohol, smoke cigarettes, and take addictive drugs to forget their problems and miseries, their tension, disappointments and failures. In place of facing their problems and making their best effort to solve them, they behave in an escaping manner. They think that the smoke of cigarettes can throw their tension away from them, and alcohol can dilute and slowly end their stress; but it is their ignorance and stupidity.

Alcohol or any chemicals can only make us sleep for a few hours or for a day, but they can never dilute and end our tension and stress. They cannot solve our difficulties and problems. Of course, if we consume more and more such materials, they can end our life, but they can never end our problems. On the contrary, they will only increase our problems and same thing happens with most of the people who cross the limit. Slowly, people become addicted of these materials and they spoil their health, life and family. They live a miserable and painful life.

What is the solution of this problem—No-addiction or Go-Addiction! Presently, on TV, we daily see advertisements of such products, where celebrities promise that their products can eradicate our addiction of tobacco, cigarette and alcohol. However, I have no experience of these products as I have never used them. Though, I have smoked cigarette (only once) and I have consumed alcohol nearly 10 times in 13 years (I had started at the age of 23), I am not addicted of anyone of them. So I do not need to go for No-addiction or Go-Addiction. Also, my wife has never advised (or scolded) me to stop drinking alcohol. So till now, I have never thought about quitting alcohol. (I have shared my experience about my smoking and alcohol in details in the next title.)

Friends, in my experience, to quit the habit of smoking and alcohol, the first and foremost thing we need is that we need to be practical. We need inner-peace and self-awareness. Understand yourself—your power and potential, and your limitations and weaknesses as well. Be strong-from-within to have patience in difficult circumstances. A sensible person can never consume any addictive materials to forget his difficulties and problems. Such a person, instead of forgetting his problems, puts his best effort to solve his problems. He succeeds or not—it does not matter, only his efforts and endurance matters. Even he fails in his efforts; he feels satisfaction in his doings. So, for such a down-to-earth person, there is no question of being addicted of smoking, alcohol and drugs. Addition of these things is nothing but committing suicide in a slow manner and a practical-person never commits suicide in any manner. He never spoils his health and life. In fact, such a person loves his health and life the most.

So, be practical, accept reality, examine your power and potential, and put your best efforts and let happen whatever happens. As you know I am also a failure in many things, but if you measure the satisfaction-level of human beings, I can stand in front of anyone on this earth, and even in the universe! So being a failure or ordinary is not a matter, the main thing is that we should be practical, sensible and strong-from-within; only then we can overcome any addiction. Additionally, here, people should understand that we can also be addicted of power, money, fame and status, so in these cases too, we need to be practical and sensible; only then we can come out of all addictions.

My Experience and Experiment with Smoking and Alcohol: As I have mentioned earlier that in 13 years of my drinking and smoking life, I have drunk nearly 10 times and I have smoked cigarette only once. Actually, I had found the taste of smoke of cigarette (Gold-flake) so bad that I had thrown it immediately. I was smoking cigarette on the advice of a friend (Mr. Hari Singh Meena from Rajasthan). At that time, I was under Fire Sub-Officer training at Ahmedabad, Gujarat. My friend had advised me that smoking makes us tension-free and relaxed. At that moment, we were in a cinema hall watching an English movie. I could not remember the name of that movie but it was a ghost-movie. Though, my friend had encouraged me a lot for smoking (his intension was good or bad, I do not know, but he was a nice guy,) I had thrown cigarette saying that I am not feeling tension-free and relaxed. Though during fire Sub-Officer training at NFSC, Nagpur, I had spent my time mostly in tension, as I was feeling very difficulty doing Left-Right and other such training exercises, yet for employment, I was ready to do everything—everything means everything!

Anyway, since I had found the taste of cigarette very bad and without any pleasure, so I said to my friend that I could not smoke it anymore in my life. After that incidence, I have never smoked. In fact, I feel smell of cigarette's smoke so bad that if someone smokes in front of me, I keep distance from him, otherwise I tell him in a requesting manner to smoke outside in open-space. Though I also want to advice every smoker that it is injurious to his (till now, I have not found any girl smoking) health and hence he should try to quit this habit, but I cannot do this; because someone may tell me—*tere baap ka kya jata hai, mera paisa meri marji, badaa aayaa hai updesh dene!* So, for a common-man, giving advice openly is dangerous. Only leaders and guru can do this job!

Previously, in my young age, I used to give such advices but most of the times, the matter goes in a wrong track and therefore I stopped giving advices openly, and started writing books. (I have already shared such a bad experience under the title 'War and Peace with Pakistan/China').

People like goody-goody talking and advices—positive talk; otherwise talk them about corrupt Indian-leaders and fraud-administrations, they will feel happy. But I am not interested to discuss only about corrupt leaders and fraud-administration to make people happy. I discuss a problem from all points of view and seek a solution of that.

I agree that most of Indian-leaders and some of government-officers and staffs are corrupt; but my question to an individual is—what are you doing here—only criticizing and complaining and making joke about them. Do you think, you will get a solution to your problem just by criticizing, complaining and making joke about them? You know the answer—the answer is a big 'NO'. You will die with your problems but you can never get solution to your problems. Only work and effort with a real and clear thinking can solve your problems and nothing else.

Now, here I would like to share my experience about drinking alcohol, as it is a very serious problem in our society. Many people are spoiling their life and family because of this addiction. Before sharing my experience, in the very beginning of it, I would like to say that I am not encouraging any one of you foı drinking alcohol. I am sharing it with you to put the reality so that you can think about this matter in a practical way. As I have mentioned that in 13 years of my drinking life, I have consumed it nearly 10 times, and this is the reason that my friends and colleagues do not count me in the drinkers-list! Once in a year (or sometimes once in two years!), when I participate in an alcohol-party, my friends ask me in surprise—Oh, you also drink! And I say, yes I also drink; but, because its taste is not good, so I drink only a little mixing it with cold-drink or fruit juice. In fact, if you put a condition that I have to drink either fruit-juice or alcohol and not both, I will prefer juice to alcohol. I have no interest to drink alcohol, and hence I mostly prefer to drink fruit juices.

Most importantly, I must say that I have never consumed alcohol to forget my problems and misery, as most of the people usually do so because of the same reason. I have always consumed it in a normal mood. I have also faced problems of poverty and unemployment and all the difficulties of life. You can imagine the difficulties and problems of a boy whose father's salary was only rupees two thousand a month. I have struggled nearly 4-5 years just to get an ordinary job to survive. But in any case, I have never consumed alcohol to forget my problems. I have always tried my best to solve my problems, otherwise—hands-up—I can't do anything more. I am not a superman or a filmy-hero who can solve every problem. No, I am a simple and common man. I have a limited power and potential. So, I do my best and finally I leave it to God. Let God do the rest. God should also do something, otherwise He will become lazy! So, I take every problem in a very practical manner.

Therefore, my sincere and friendly advice to you is that, if you are in a problem or difficulty; think a way-out of it; make effort to come out of it. Smoking cigarettes and consuming alcohol and drugs cannot show us ways; instead they block our thinking and ways and slowly kill us. I am saying this with my own experience, because once I had drunk a lot just to check what happens when we drink a lot. In a party, I had drunk nearly a bottle of MacDowell whisky within 7 to 10 minutes and I had started feeling uneasiness and vomiting. I was not feeling any enjoyment or happiness, as people describe their experience about this matter in this way. Instead, I was feeling disturbed and my thinking was nearly blocked! I was not able to think in a proper manner.

I was feeling that if I would stand and walk, I may fall at any moment. I was so disturbed that I could not have my dinner at that night. After party, with difficulty, I had come to my home and said to my wife—I am not feeling well and I am going to sleep. But where is sleep! Nearly after 2 hours I had gone into sleep. Till now, my wife had never scolded me for drinking but that night she had scolded me a little.

That night, really I was surprised thinking that a bottle of alcohol is so powerful that it can overpower me. It can make me weak, uneasy and disturbed. But it was a reality and I had accepted it. Thereafter, I had decided that in future, I will never do this experiment with me.

3 years have been gone to that incidence—Dec 2010. We had celebrated that party for getting promotion after 10 years of our joining service. Comparing to our seniors, we had got promotion 7 to 10 years earlier and we were happy! Like our government, our promotion is also very slow but our job is safe and that is a matter of great satisfaction in the present bad scenario of private sectors. Most of employees are disturbed thinking that they may be fired at any moment. I was also in the same position while working at Oswal Chemical and Fertilizers Ltd., Paradeep, Orissa. Really, it is a very frustrating thing to be treated in a use-and-throw manner and therefore I came in a government job. Less payment is OK but tension and use-and-throw behavior—I cannot tolerate it. So friends, be practical, accept realities, test your potential, and put your best efforts to solve your problem and let happen whatever happens. Never go for drinking in a nervous and tension mood and then see how you can overcome your every addiction.

How Long Could We Ignore Our Problems?: Friends, we can ignore our problems and difficulties with our false beliefs and blaming-others-attitude. We can ignore them believing in our poor luck, fate and destiny. We can ignore them indulging ourselves in gossips, rumors, news, TV and film, fun and entertainments. We can ignore them consuming alcohol and drugs because most of people get good-sleep after consuming these chemicals. We can ignore them blaming our society and systems—leaders and government and their policies, police, laws and orders, constitution, lawyers and judges etc.

However, the eternal question is—how long could we ignore our problems; how long could we hope and give false-consolation to ourselves; how long could we ignore the ground realities—for one life, for two lives…, for ten lives… how long? How many lives we could live a stressful and a miserable life and die in hell? Do you want to live such lives life-long! Think and ask yourself—because there is an 'entity' within you, within everyone—which can reply you and that entity is—your inner-sensibility, inner-awareness. Stop asking others—leaders, gurus, gods, teachers, fortunetellers… No; ask your inner-self. You have asked others for centuries, for many lives, now it is time to ask your inner-self. If God is within everyone; why to ask others, why to believe-in any guru, god or leader? No, stop this believing and trust, and ask within yourself.

In fact, asking others and believing their words is the basic cause of our poor understanding, sensibility and conscience. We are ignorant and downtrodden only because of belief and trust on gurus, gods and leaders. Therefore, now we should ask our inner-self, our inner-God. Awake your inner-God. Your inner-God will reply your every question of life. I ask every important question to my inner-God and He replies me; and in fact, through my writings,

I share the same reply with you. So, you also increase your inner-peace and ask your inner-God. God will give you the best reply and the best solution of your every problem.

✌

8
Prove India Is World-Guru!

Are We Really World-Guru?

We hear that once upon a time, India was a world-guru. India was most powerful, intelligent, and prosperous in the world. India was a golden-bird. All beautiful adjectives were true for India. If it is so, why India is in such a poor and downtrodden condition at present? Why India is standing in poverty, unemployment, huge-population, illiteracy, malnutrition, pollution, fraud and corruption, and many other problems? And, what a contradiction, world-guru is standing in problems and his disciples are developing—some have been already developed! Guru is crying and weeping and disciples are enjoying and laughing—what a scene!

Does not it show that we are world-guru only for namesake? We are phony world-guru and not real world-guru. Yes, it is so; and if it is not, we have to prove it wrong by changing and developing India. Guru, God and government have been proved failure to develop India. Now, this responsibility has come to the shoulders of common men. So, we, the common men, have to take this responsibility and we have to prove India a world-guru again.

Move like a Joint-Family: All gurus and gods of India (and even of world) have taught and inspired us one basic thing—live like a joint-family, live and let live; so that we can develop one-and-all. However, due to lack of understanding, we did not understand their teachings and we created many religions, classes, castes and isms in their names and teachings. We created differences and discrimination among us. So, basically, creating discrimination in the name of religions and castes is our fault and not that of our olden gurus and gods.

But now, we can understand their virtuous teachings in a better way as today we are more educated, logical and sensible. Friends, here I strongly feel to say that the most important thing to feel their virtuous teachings is—we need a heart and not a mind, we need sensibility and not knowledge. Even an illiterate Kabir can understand their virtuous teachings—and not only can understand but also teach us; but a PhD without a live-heart and sensibility cannot feel their teachings—this is the difficulty of human-psychology. So, we need a live-heart and sensibility—only this can make us aware of their virtuous teachings and only this can motivate us to unite and make efforts to develop as a joint-family.

God Is Crying for Our Help to Develop India!: India is in such a poor and downtrodden condition that even God needs our help to develop India. Without help and support of common men, and especially youths of India, God is helpless. He can do nothing. Surely, most of people of India will be surprised to hear that God needs our help, because from the ancient history, we have learnt that God is the most powerful body and He can do everything. Nothing is impossible for God. He can finish our every problem within a moment—we just need praying and praising Him! But sadly, this is only a belief—a holy but phony belief.

Reality is that, God is as normal as we are. God has not any special and supernatural power. God is made up of atoms and every atom is normal and ordinary. Of course, God has billions and billions of hydrogen bombs, but hydrogen bombs cannot solve our problems. Hydrogen bombs cannot eradicate poverty, unemployment, illiteracy, malnutrition, pollution, corruption etc. Yes, God can control population if He would drop some hydrogen bombs from sun on earth! But, the matter is, God has not given us birth to kill us, instead He has given us birth to grow and develop. So, God is very powerful, I agreed, but He cannot solve our root-level problems with that power.

For that, He needs our help. He needs our understanding and sensibility. He needs our work and efforts. Therefore, help God in whatever way you can help Him—little or large, it does not matter, just help Him. In addition, please stop praying and praising and giving donations to God to complete your job. Do not treat God as an agent or a middleman. You know, I never pray God—I talk God but never pray Him. I talk to my inner-self (soul) from where God is connected.

Though, in this life, I am a born-poor and I have faced many scarcities. But I have never prayed God to fulfill my requirements. In this regard, my logic is very simple—God is not a fool whom I need to say to do this or do that. God must be virtuous and intelligent. So He must know very well what He needs do. So, God is doing what He needs to do; now it is our turn to do what we need to do; and already I have discussed what we need to do to change and develop India.

To sum up, I just want to say that without help and support of common men, God is helpless. So, if we want to change and develop India we must all need to make effort and work with understanding and sensibility.

God Is Purely Fair and Lovely: The findings of modern science prove that nature is purely fair and crystal-clear. The elementary particles of nature like atoms and electrons are purely fair and unbiased. For instance, everyone is same for an electron. An electron does not care—who is who or what. One may be a top-level scientist but it gives him the same electric-shock what it gives to an illiterate person. It does not differentiate between both of them. This clearly shows that nature and existence are purely fair and unbiased.

In fact, this is the reason why in spirituality, it is said that everyone is same in the 'eye' of God, and that God is our nature and existence. Here, we should also be aware that the intrinsic virtue of elementary particles does not change with time. An electron does not change with time, it is always same. And this fact shows that this existence is fair and unbiased from the eternity and it will always remain same.

Futhermore, being an unbiased and fair body, our God is caring and lovely as well. You may have also heard that time is a great pain-balm and time can heal our every wound. But, it is not the actual reality. The actual reality is that it is not time but the healing-virtue of nature that heals our wounds. If there had been no healing-virtue in nature, our wounds could have never been healed. We had been waiting till the end of our life but our wounds had remained same; they could not be healed.

This healing virtue of nature shows the caring and loving virtue of nature and existence, which is our real God. So, our God loves and cares us like a mother. In fact, the basic aim of our God behind our creation is to care and develop us so that we may be able to emerge our in-built virtue which it has been developing within us from eternity.

Our God Is Highly Active, Awakened and Self-Determined: Though our God is fair, lovely and caring like a mother, its love and care is not blind. I am saying this because some of mothers blindly love their children, which is not good for carrier and future of their children. However, God does not love and care us blindly. God is highly active, awaken, and sensible and He loves and cares us in the same manner. Science proves that in nature and existence—nothing happens by a chance; everything happens due to a certain cause. Action-reaction and cause and effect always go together. Each step of a natural particle is calculated and self-determined—self-determined means we cannot move them as per our own wish and desire. They are not under our control. They are self-controlled.

Even the top scientist of the world cannot move even an electron as per his own wish and desire, and in fact, this is the practical meaning of Heisenberg's Uncertainty Principle. So, all natural particles are self-controlled and self-director. Additionally, natural particles are very active and responsive. They are so active that they never take rest even for a moment. We and other living beings sleep and take rest but they never take rest. They work continuously day and night. They are actual 24X7 workers. Even during our sleep, they work and in fact, we are alive only because they work day and night. In case, if they would stop working continuously, we would die instantly. If iron and hemoglobin would start taking rest and stop oxygen supply to our organs, we would die within a few minutes.

Also, it is an interesting thing to observe that during our sleep, we become like a dead body. We become absent from our body. However again we become present in our body after nearly 6-8 hours. How does it happen? It happens because the micro particles of our body like molecules, ions, atoms and electrons are always in action. They never take rest. In addition, we should understand that we see a dream only because the electrons of our mind always remain active. They do not take rest with us.

However, we should understand that the main job of electrons of brain is to make us alive and active and not to create a film to show us at night. In fact, electrons create a film only because we are very filmy and showy in our real life. We are all ordinary and common men, but we show others as if we were extra-ordinary and special. Like filmy actors, we also show our acting in our real life and this fake acting creates a film, which we see in night while sleeping. Thus, we see, how natural particles and hence God is very active, awaken and responsive.

We Need Change and Not God: Friends, we should understand this fact that a theory of science may be modified and changed, but the intrinsic virtue of a natural particle can never be changed. Many theories have been modified and changed with time, but the virtue of a natural particle has never been changed. An atom is still an atom in its eternal shape and virtue. In fact, there is no impurity or drawback in nature and existence (the real God), so there is no need to change in them. The principles of atomic structure of scientists like Rutherford and Niels Bohr can have drawbacks and hence they can be modified and changed, but the basic structure of an atom can never be changed. Besides, in nature and existence, everywhere we see a harmony among natural bodies. This shows that every particle has an inbuilt awareness to move and act, and this shows greatness of creator God.

From the above fact, I want to say that for change and development, we need change in ourselves and not in nature and existence. We need change in our thinking and behaviour. We need to think for one and all. Besides, we need change in our life-style knowing the virtues of natural particles. We should not try and pray to God to change nature as per our own comforts and convenience. To put this fact in simple and practical terms, I want to say that if you smoke cigarette and drink alcohol and pray to God—please save me from lungs-cancer and liver-problem and save my life! What God can do? Nothing, He will just raise His hands. He will be helpless. He can only scream and cry for you within you (soul), but He can do nothing. You will get lungs-cancer and liver-problem and ultimately you will die—not a natural death but a self-wished (*meri marji*) death!

I am saying this because, even after knowing that smoking cigarette and drinking alcohol are injurious to health, you have smoked cigarette and consumed alcohol. So, basically you yourself are responsible for your death. In addition, you should understand that because of these diseases, your life will be more painful and miserable. So, indirectly God is saving you from a painful and miserable life. So, try to understand God's thinking and working! Of course, God can give you birth again but He cannot save you with lungs-cancer and damaged-liver, it is sure.

Friends, reality is that God always loves and cares us, but we rarely feel His love and care. We are so selfish and we are so hunger for money, power and status that in front of God we always stand like a beggar—we pray like a beggar! We rarely say to God with full heart and soul (*dil se*)—thank you for whatever good things you have done for me. Of course, you can also hate God occasionally, if you feel that God is doing wrong with you, but you should also feel thankful to God for good things in your life.

Treat God as your friend—the best friend. This is the way I treat God. But we selfish people—take credit of good things on ourselves and give credit of bad things to God—and government! Whatever bad things happen in our life, it happens because of our God or Government or Guru or Guardian (4Gs!). For every wrong and mistake these 4Gs are responsible and blamable—this is our thinking. Friends, we must change this thinking. We must be practical and we must take responsibility of our life. We have born with our own desires and wishes, so we must take responsibility of our life, only then we can change our life.

We are Responsible for Our Problems and Not God: It is a great observation of religion and spirituality that—whatever happens, it happens for good. Perhaps, first time, lord Sri Krishna had declared this fact as he is very well known for this declaration; however I consider that this the basic essence of all religions and spirituality. And in modern science context, in place of saying this, it is better to say—whatever happens, it happens for balance and coordination; because it is the observation of science that in nature, whatever happens, it happens for balance and coordination. Every atom reacts with another atom to be more balanced and stable. Every electron changes its location, speed, momentum and even its form (mass into energy and vice-versa) to be more balanced and stable. Therefore, our creator-existence is continuously in action at the deepest possible level for balance, coordination and development, and any sensible and intelligent being can easily observe this truth.

Someone may ask that if God does everything for balance, coordination and development then why we are facing so many difficulties and problems. Why we have illiteracy, poverty, unemployment, population-explosion, hunger, malnutrition, corruption, pollution, violence, injustice and many others. Who is responsible for these problems? You may feel annoyed hearing the answer, but reality is that for all these problems, we are responsible.

Our ego, ignorance, cleverness, cunningness, corruptness and over-smartness are responsible. Read science and you will know that an atom never does anything bad and biased with anyone and our God is nothing but a big molecule rather the biggest molecule made up of different kinds of atoms. So our God never does anything bad and biased. Therefore, we must accept that for all human and social problems we are responsible and not God. And if we want to come out of these problems, we must change and develop our thinking and awareness. We must rise above our selfishness and I & my mentality and we should think for one and all. We should help and support one another like friends—this is the only way to solve our problems.

Remember, simply blaming and criticizing God and government are not going to solve our problems. We have blamed and criticized them for centuries. In past, in place of blaming government and leaders, we used to blame kings and their ministers; but our problems did not solve. Therefore, we should leave this blaming attitude and think and act in a supporting manner. Both government and people should work in a supporting manner, only then we can change India. Otherwise, even after thousands of years, problems will remain same.

World-famous leaders, social-reformers, gurus and gods will come and go (many have already come and gone!), but problems will always remain same. With my saying, please do not understand that there is fault in sincere leaders and gurus; there is fault in people like Gandhi and Gautama Buddha. No, they have not faults and there is no doubt about their sincerity and efforts. Actually fault is within us and that fault is our selfishness, ego and ignorance. So, think with a broad view—think about India, think about one and all, think about total humanity, then you will think in a proper manner. Therefore, we must think and act in a helping and supporting manner, only then we can develop a healthy and prosperous India.

God Is Not Hidden—We Just Need an Eye To See Him!: You may have also heard this saying that God is hidden from us because He fears that if He would come in front of us; we will all start begging and crying to fulfill our desires and dreams. To fulfill one's desires and demands, one may go on hunger-strike and someone may warn to commit suicide! In such a critical situation, God will become very upset and disturbed and therefore, He does not want to come in front of us.

But the question is, contrary to this thinking, we also believe that God is very merciful, powerful and great. He can do anything and everything in a moment. Then this question rises that how such a powerful and merciful God can be feared and hidden from us? Obviously not; such a powerful God can never be feared and hidden, and hence He will surely come in front of us. But He is not coming! We fought First and Second World Wars and we are preparing for the third one, but still God is not coming. At present, we are facing so many problems and difficulties not only in India but all over the world, but still God is not coming. And I am 100% sure that God will never come—we can wait for Him till eternity, but He will never come; why? Because, God is not somewhere in the sky and He is not feared and hidden from us, but He (the existence) is here in front of us.

We just need an eye to see Him and that eye is the eye of self-awareness. People like Jesus, Sri Krishna, Gautama Buddha, Kabir etc. have the same eye and they have seen the same existence as God. You study their words carefully, they have all described this existence as God—the Creator. And, this God is rigidly and boldly standing in front of us. Anyone can cry at the top of his voice, and anyone can do anything to satisfy his desire. But, Creator-existence never fears with anyone. How can it fear—it has trillions and trillions of Hydrogen bombs, and just 100 Hydrogen bombs are enough to destroy the whole world in a moment of time. It can kill even the strongest and the most powerful person of the world within no time; and for that, a hydrogen bomb is not required, but just a tiny bullet is enough! So, there is no question of fearing for God. And here, I have talked in a bullet-manner only because we have created many false beliefs about God. So, only such a bullet talking can eradicate our false beliefs about God and not goody-goody bogus and useless beliefs and sayings.

Therefore, start doing whatever you want to do, because only your doing (effort) can fulfill your desires and dreams. You have prayed and praised God for many lives but still your desires are unfulfilled; now it is time to work and make efforts. What I have done in my life—I have just made effort and still I have continued it. I don't think about result. I just do what I feel. I never leave doing and making effort. I am here to make effort and nothing else. Making efforts gives me inner satisfaction and peace, and I want to convey the same message to one and all, and especially to youths of India. So, come out of false-beliefs about God and make efforts to fulfill your desires and dreams, only this can change you and India.

God Is Not Just a Belief or Story But a Reality:

People have made God just a goody-goody story and they have been discussing this story for a long time. But, what is the use of such stories and discussions—nothing, just time-pass! People—and especially old and retired people have extra time and they do not know what to do with their extra time, so they pass their extra time in such useless stories. I can firmly say that all such stories and discussions are useless and absurd. Hence, finish all these stories and experience the real God by emerging your inner-virtue and potential. The real God resides within you in your potential.

Workout and emerge your potential and make alive your inner-God. I experience God without any stories and discussions. I don't do any religious formalities with God. Also, I have never taken advices or blessings of any guru and god-man. I have experienced God with my own understanding, awareness and efforts. And, if someone—especially a guru or god-man, thinks that I have no experience of God and I need his experience and guidance, then I am ready to meet and discuss this matter with him—with anyone—whatever he or she may be. He or she may be a guru or god-man in the eye of world, but I shall treat him as a common man. I shall meet him as a friend. I consider even God as my friend, so there is no question of treating a human being like a guru or god-man.

Once, it had happened that I was reading Rajneesh (OSHO) and I was reading him with such a great interest that a friend had remarked on me, "Now, I would also become a disciple of Rajneesh". At that time, I was only 16 years old and I was preparing for engineering-competitions—to be an IITian was also my dream. Hearing my friend's remark, for first time, I had ignored his remark, but when he had repeated his same remark for the second and third time, (the book had nearly 500 pages—*Sambhog Se Samadhi Ki Oar*(!), so it took nearly two days to read it. Though a teenager is not advised to read such a title, I have never restricted myself to read or see or hear anything. I am little bit against Gandhi's three monkeys! I am always ready and available to experience everything!)

I had replied, "I could never be disciple of anyone, whoever may be this anyone." Not only this, I had also told him, "If Rajneesh is interested to become my disciple, it is his wish! Otherwise I can never be disciple of anyone." And though, at that time, I was a teenager, "something" was there within me due to which I had said these words, and that "something" was a certain level of my inner-awakening—which I had acquired in this life by-birth!

So, though I am a common man, I am ready to discuss any matter related to God, religion or spirituality, and most importantly, issues related to human and social development with anyone of this world. He or she may be a guru, god-man, leader, social reformer, scientist, or the most-intelligent person of the world (I don't know his name as I could not find it on Google!), or anyone in this universe.

In fact, I discuss this matter with real God—through my awakening-soul, so I can easily discuss this matter with anyone of the universe. And, I want to say the same thing to everyone and especially to every youth of India—'Treat everyone as a friend and never become a follower or disciple of anyone. Use your own conscience and sensibility about right and wrong and take decision yourself.' Put your own sensibility and sincere-effort for your development. Remember, even a tiny atom is a self-director, so why can't we, certainly we can.

Don't Go In Search of God—Let Him Come To Meet You!: Is there anyone on this earth, who can tell me the exact address of God? I want to tell this address to the whole world. Everyone wants to meet God, so I want to message this address to everyone. The body which I consider as God is this existence and in this book, I have mentioned Him in details. But common men have a different thinking and belief about God and hence I have asked the above question, that is, the exact address of God.

It is said that God is our father and He is such a great knowledgeable father that He knows everything. He knows each and every corner of the universe. He knows from centre to the circumference of universe. He knows from tiny atom to the large Black-hole. What a fantastic knowledgeable God! But the question is, if God is such a knowledgeable and intelligent body, then why we need to go in search of such an intelligent body? In case, if someone losses somewhere in the universe, God can easily search him. He can find him in a second rather in a micro-second! Moreover, it is father's duty and responsibility to search for his child and not His child's duty; because a child is child and hence he is immature, so he can be lost somewhere.

Once it happened that my son was missing from his school. I asked the school-bus driver, he had no idea about it. I had asked the school-authority, they had also not any instant reply. I scolded them and warned them for a police complaint if they would not be able to find him within a few minutes. Thereafter, I had thought to go to the school and I had started my journey in the same school bus as it was returning to school. During journey to the school, I was always in contact with the school-authority.

The whole scene was looking like a filmy-drama. But I was a little-upset (anyone would be). After nearly 10 minutes of drama, it so happened that just before reaching the school, the school-authority had found the exact information about my son. My son had come to home with my neighbour and had stayed at neighbour's house! And in short, this incident had been happened due to misunderstanding of many people including my son, and basically, my son was the main culprit.

But, he is a child (at that time, he was only 9 years old) and hence immature and therefore, he can do such a mistake.

From this incident, I want to say that it is the father's duty to search for his child and not his child's duty. A child may be careless and negligent but a father should never be careless and negligent. And, in the above incidence, my child was enjoying watching TV and eating snacks at my neighbour's house without caring that his father was so worried about him. Friends, exactly same thing is happening between our God and us.

Our God (please know that God is not only father but mother as well, and in my consideration, God is more mother than father, He is more feminine than masculine.) is always in search of us. God is always trying to make contact with us. He is trying to contact us through our soul—through our inner-feelings. He is always trying to motivate and guide us to move on the right path—the path of peace, prosperity and enlightenment. But due to lack of sensibility and self-awakening, we are not caring our inner-feelings and search God here and there. So, basically we need self-awakening and inner-peace to know and feel God and for that we need to practice meditation.

Apart from this, it is also important to note that, basically, we do not search for God, but we search for a Fraud, who can take something like money or gold from us and can fulfill our desires in a magical way. And because of this very magic-mentality of ours, we have created fraud-market in the name of God. Some people like guru and god-man, show us goody-goody dreams in the name of God and in return they enjoy a luxurious life on our hard-earnings. Such people behave as if they were agents of God.

However, these agents do not know the real-God and therefore they play such tricks. When they will know the real God, they will stop playing such tricks. But, because of poverty and unemployment problem, I am not sure that they will stop it! Poverty and unemployment are converting many normal people into fraud and corrupt people. However, if we want to close this fraud-market, we should increase our level of knowledge, awareness and sensibility (especially about science and technology). Only our knowledge, awareness and sensibility can save us from this fraud-market.

As you know I have never gone in search of God. I have never met any guru or god-man. I have never done any religious formalities with God, and I have always discarded goody-goody beliefs and stories about God. Yet, see, the real God—the compassionate creator-existence met me, He contacted me. He brought me on the right path—the path on which I find the true meaning of my life.

In fact, from very beginning of my life, God was trying to make a contact with me but it was only me who was avoiding his calls and guidance. However, God is compassionate and hence he never left his hopes and efforts. He always continued his efforts and ultimately succeeded in making a strong connection with me. He succeeded in motivating and guiding me to move in the right direction and this book is the result of His same guidance. That's why I dedicate my every book to God—the creator.

It is not just a formality but it is a reality—it is my real emotion and dedication towards the creator-existence. I have dedicated this book to the common-men and youths of India and it is also the wish of God. Therefore, God does the duty of a responsible father, it is only we who neglect and avoid our duty and responsibility. So, please allow God to contact you through your soul, through your inner-feelings so that He can guide you as He guides me.

Agents of God–"Be Careful!": In the above title, I have talked about fraud-market in the name of God. This paragraph is for those people who are in this fraud-market.

Dear friends, (for me, all are friends!) please be aware that, today you may be a guru or god-man in the eye of common men, but tomorrow or in your next birth you may become a slumdog. God is mixing-up all of us to give opportunity for development to all of us. Therefore, today if you have become a guru or god-man and have cheated crores of money from your followers and disciples; then be prepared to become a slumdog in your next birth, as God may give you birth as a slumdog to check your level of cunningness and cleverness!

We get more opportunities to check our level of cunningness and cleverness in a poor and slum family than in a rich and wealthy family. I also got such opportunities only because of my poverty (I may have also cheated people in my past lives! But in present life, I have forgotten them due to my poor memory!). And remember, the same people, who at present treat you as a guru or god-man will treat you as a slumdog, because at that time, your face-value and personality will be changed. No one can recognize you with your past face-value. At that time, you will become an ordinary slumdog and people will treat you in the same way as they treat other slumdogs.

In the present life, I myself have lived in poverty and I know how these people treat with poor and slum-dogs. I have seen how people differentiate and discriminate others as per his power, property and status. Therefore friends, everyone is a friend for me; there is no enemy in the whole of universe. Everyone is a unique creation of creator-existence and hence everyone is its child, so we are all friends. So friends, I request you to stop all cheating and fraud activities in the name of God and religion. Be sensible and do some job/work to earn money and live peacefully and happily without any burden of cheating and fraud on your soul. Otherwise, be prepared to face the challenges of becoming a slumdog! At that time, don't blame God for making you a slumdog!

Beware! Life-cycle mechanism is not just a bogus spiritual-theory but a reality, and science is going to prove this reality very soon. Science has completed 90% task in this regard, only 10% task has been left to prove the reality of life-cycle. Science will very soon trace and determine the trajectory of soul in the same way as it traces and determines the trajectory of a rocket and satellite.

We are All Friends and Not Hindu, Muslim, Sikh, Christian etc.: No any atom, molecule or natural body belongs to any caste and religion. An atom is neither a Hindu nor a Muslim, it is just an atom—a mixture of mass and energy. Our body is also a molecule made-up of atoms like carbon, hydrogen, oxygen and others. So, our body is a nature-made molecule and hence it has no relation with any man-made class-system like caste and religion.

In fact, our class-systems have been created due to lack of awareness of common people; otherwise people like Sri Krishna, Mohammad, Guru Nanak and Jesus had no intension to create and establish such class-systems in their names and teachings. They had only one intension and that is, to develop people, to develop humanity, to develop one-and-all. Hence, it is only our ignorance and foolishness to create differences and discriminations among ourselves in their names and teachings.

Most importantly, our Creator-existence wants to keep a direct relation with us. It does not want any caste and religious system to contact us. It does not want any guru, god-man or a mediator to talk us. It stimulates and guides us directly through our soul. 'What is right and what is wrong' the Creator tells us directly through our soul in a little-voice. We just need inner-peace to listen to our inner-voice. Therefore, all myths and beliefs about caste and religious systems which we have stored in our mind are nothing but false beliefs and stories. We have to come out of those false stories and only science and self-awareness can give us power to come out of those false stories and beliefs.

Only Science and Sensibility Can Root Out Our Religious-Differences: When a person takes a new birth, he forgets everything of his past-life. Nature erases every unwanted thing from his mind, and belief about caste and religious differences is an unwanted thing. There is no use of any caste and class system in our human society. So, if a child takes a new birth, he takes birth with a new brain having no differences of caste and class system. Now this question raises that who teaches our children about differences of castes and religions?

Who teaches them which is a lower caste and which is a higher caste? Obviously, we are the people who teach them these differences, because no one comes from sky to teach them these differences. Again, the next question raises that why most of the children easily learn and accepted these differences (beliefs), and the answer is—lack of their self-awareness.

Due to lack of self-awareness and sensibility, a child easily accepts his parental and social beliefs, customs and traditions. He does not argue and does not ask why and how. He easily becomes a stereotype and a yes-boss type person. On the contrary, a soul with awareness and sensibility does not accept anyone and anything so easily. He reasons, observes and judges the reality himself, and unless he satisfies himself, he does not accept anyone—anyone means anyone—whoever may be this anyone. Whole world may consider a person as a leader, guru, or even a god, but he does not accept and follow this person so easily. This is the virtue and power of self-awareness. If I have not accepted such false beliefs, it is only because of my self-awareness, which I have acquired in this life by-birth. And, I am writing only because of the same virtue of my being; and through my writing, I want to create and develop the same virtue in everyone, because only this can root out our all differences of castes, classes and religions.

The Psychology of Heaven and Hell: People believe that somewhere in the sky, there is a heaven and hell. A person who does a good work goes to heaven and enjoys a luxurious life; and reversely, a person who does a bad work goes to hell and gets punishments there. I hope I will go to both of these places—first to hell and then to heaven, as in first half of my life—during poverty and unemployment, I have done some bad works and in second half, I am doing some good works. No problem, I will get experience of both! However, I consider that the concept of God, heaven and hell are only illusions created by our gurus and gods to motivate people to do good works and avoid bad works. Otherwise, there is no heaven and hell in the whole of universe.

There is no God sitting above in the sky to give us pleasure for our good works and punishment for our bad works. And that's why modern scientists who have discovered invisible X-ray and black-hole could not succeeded to discover heaven, hell and God. In fact, the thing which does not exist how anyone can discover it. No, no one can do it. And therefore,

I am 100% sure that even after thousands of years (if III World-War does not happen and our earth remains safe from global warming!), scientists could never be able to discover heaven, hell and God (that God, about which people dream and imagine, otherwise the real God, that is, existence is always in front of us. There is no need to search this God.)

The feeling of happiness or sorrow is nothing but reaction of our own action, and we get this reaction at the very same moment of action. We don't get it prior to or later of our action. Atoms and electrons react at the very same moment. They do not wait to react. They have no mind to think and wait and watch. They just react like a robot—programmed by nature, and they react in a tit-for-tat manner. For instance, if we eat sweets we feel sweetness of sweet at the very same moment. We do not feel it prior or latter of eating. We may dream about its taste at any time, but that is only a dream, that is not reality. Similarly, if we eat poison, we would not die tomorrow but we die instantly (it also depends upon the power of poison!). So, this matter is very simple and practical to understand. In simple terms, we can also say that: act good and get reaction good; act bad and get reaction bad; otherwise we can say, do good feel good, and do bad feel bad. Therefore, we create and experience our heaven and hell at the very same moment and at the very same earth. We don't go anywhere in the sky to experience it.

Though the intention of our gurus and gods behind creating the concept of God, heaven and hell was holy and good, with the progress of science and technology, people started discarding such beliefs as science proved them wrong. And subsequently, people started doing whatever they wanted to do without thinking about going to heaven or hell, or meeting God. At present, only illiterate people fear somewhat from the belief of God, heaven and hell; otherwise modern educated people have no fear from these beliefs. For them, even God is an outdated and obsolete thing. They don't care God. They care and fear somewhat police and laws but not God. They do whatever they like—right or wrong, they themselves judge it.

However, modern and educated people should understand that though there is no God and heaven and hell in the universe, there is a deep-level organizing force working in the existence. Due to this very organizing force, at present, a little part of this earth looks like a heaven; otherwise once upon a time, this earth was a hell. It was a dead planet like moon and other planets. So, this deserted and dead-planet became an alive-planet only because of the creative effort of the creator existence. Of course, we are also a part of this creative effort, but creator existence is the actual source of this effort.

A person like Isaac Newton, Thomas Alva Edition and Albert Einstein cannot be produced by a couple in an overnight; rather they can be produced only by the creator-existence after a long period of action and reactions of DNA-chemicals! Therefore, come out of this belief that there is no organizing-force working in the nature and existence. Besides, I have already mentioned that no one can cheat nature and existence (the real God). We can cheat one another, we can play hide-and-seek or cat-and-mouse game with one another, but we can never play this game with creator-existence. We are all opened and in fact 'naked' in front of God. So never think to play hide-and-seek game with God.

Therefore, if you do a bad or unsocial activity, you will not go to hell, but you will get reaction (pain and misery) of your action on this very earth, otherwise you will again take birth to correct your mistake and face the consequences. I think,

I have also taken birth to correct my own past mistakes, but what are my past-mistakes, I have no idea about it! I have never made effort to go in my past life to know my good and bad doings or works. I have no time and interest to do this activity. I have interest only in present—now. Past is like a dead thing for me, there is no use of making a dead thing alive. There is no use of counting bones of skeleton-of-past. So let died be dead.

Hence, 'as you sow so shall you reap' is sure, and even modern science justifies it. In present modern science age, we can easily discard beliefs about heaven, hell and God; but we must not forget that we must get reaction of our action. We must face the consequences of our action in one way or the other. Therefore, we should all stop illegal and unsocial activities and we should all make effort to create a heaven on this earth. We should help to transform our earth into a heaven so that we will always take birth in a heaven, and never in the hell of poverty, unemployment and other social evils.

Like Our God, Think Development for One-And-All: The creator-existence is very fair and democratic and in true sense, only creator is fair and real democratic; otherwise, we people are very phony and fake democratic. We talk about equality and justice, but everywhere we create in-equality, injustice and discrimination. We say and show something and do something else. However, for existence, we are all its children and hence without any biasness and discrimination, it provides opportunity to everyone for growth and development.

To provide opportunity to everyone, it has a mechanism which—in spirituality—popularly known as life-cycle mechanism (for details, read my book—How to Develop One and All, at my website). Through this mechanism, this existence provides opportunity to everyone for growth and development. This mechanism has been working from eternity and it will continue to work forever. Therefore, for one's misery and problems, if someone blames only nature and God, then it shows only his stupidity and ignorance and nothing else.

How this existence works, here we understand this matter with the real-life examples of two great and intelligent souls. As we know, Siddhartha (latter known as Gautama Buddha), was born in a rich and prosperous family. He was a prince and he had enjoyed a rich and luxurious life. After being fully satisfied and content living a luxurious life, he had gone to jungle in search of something like self-realization, eternal-peace, truth, enlightenment etc. This event seems very simple and ordinary—there is no peculiarity in this event. In fact, it should happen with most of the rich people, but it does not happen—it is another issue.

However friends, what about Kabir Das!? Whether he was born in a rich family? Had he enjoyed a luxurious life? Such a misery happened in the very beginning of his life that even his mother had left him somewhere alone after giving him birth. He might have been died within a few hours if someone had not taken care of him. If you feel this event with your heart and soul, your eyes may tears like mine. Even his caring parents were very simple and ordinary men. They were poor and illiterate weaver and hence Kabir Das also become an illiterate weaver. In spite of these all difficulties and hardships, Kabir Das had developed as a rich and intelligent soul. In my awareness, he is one of the most intelligent souls of this planet. I have great rather the greatest respect for this soul.

Now, we ponder over the above facts that how Kabir Das had developed as a rich and intelligent soul. How such an ordinary and illiterate person can speak such beautiful and vibrant words, like '*pothi padh-padh jag muaa, pundit bhayaa na koy, dhaayee akshar prem ka padhe so pandit hoy*', to create love, compassion and awakening in people? He has spoken thousands of such beautiful poetries. How? We simply say, it is a matter of God-gift and stop the matter. But it is not the actual reality. To understand the actual reality, we should understand the life-cycle mechanism.

In fact, in Kabir Das's case, life-cycle mechanism has been worked and proved fruitful. Actually, this mechanism has been working in everyone's life, but everyone is not making sincere effort for his development and hence our society and humanity is in such a bad and downtrodden condition. Sincerity is missing in our life. We are mostly playing blame-game. In addition, we are using our mind only for gaining more and more money, power and status without applying our heart and soul—our feelings and inner-voice.

I want to present this fact more clearly by taking consideration of Kabir Das's life: in fact, in the past lives, when the creator-existence had given birth to Kabir Das in a rich and prosperous family, he had utilized that opportunity in developing his wisdom and conscience. He had not only enjoyed a luxurious life and added more wealth and currency in his parent's bank account; but he had also made effort for his own growth and development. He had made effort to gain knowledge and awareness and we see this awareness in his next birth, that is, when he was known as Kabir Das. His virtuous and awakening words clearly shows that he had a deep-experience of life. Without life-cycle mechanism, such a surprising event can never be happened.

Thus, the creator existence makes a genuine effort for development of everyone—one and all. It loves and cares everyone. It gives opportunity to everyone. However, it is the individual's responsibility to utilize the provided opportunity. Existence or God is not a person who may come in front of us and say, "Do this and do that". No, God is not a person but it is the whole existence. God surrounds us from every side. We are all like cells in the God's huge body, and we are all connected to God through our souls, through our inner-feelings. So whatever God wants to tell us, He tells us through our inner-feelings. Now it is our responsibility to listen to our inner-feelings and act and move accordingly.

Here, we should also understand that in the case of Siddhartha and Kabir Das, for a Siddhartha, it was not a difficult task to be awakened, but for a Kabir Das it was really a difficult task. Prosperity may transform a Siddhartha into a Buddha—an awakened-soul, but poverty rarely transforms a Kabir into an intelligent and awakened-soul, and therefore, I have great respect for Kabir Das. Though Kabir Das is not considered as a guru or messiah for humanity like Gautama Buddha or Sri Krishna, yet I have the greatest respect for this awakened soul.

Therefore friends, we should utilize and work-out our potential to our level best. If someone thinks that he is not getting an opportunity for growth, he should create it with his own hard-work and effort. If you cannot create a 'door' of opportunity, at least you should create a window or even a tiny-hole, through which you can get a chance to develop and progress.

If you think that, at a sudden, one day you will get a big opportunity, then rarely you will get such an opportunity. And, it is possible that you may wait for a big opportunity life-long and you may die without getting it! So, instead of wasting your time in waiting, you should start creating a tiny-hole of opportunity. Slowly you turn that hole into a window and then into a door.

Our life is for this—making efforts—thinking, planning and working; adding, deleting, editing, creating… and moving further and further in our life. Even at the end of your life, if you feel that 'something' has been left to do, existence will give you opportunity to do that. Existence is very compassionate. In fact, existence feels happy that someone of its children wants to carry forward his virtuous work further and further for development of people and humanity. So, existence feels gratitude towards you. It thanks you.

Our life is not a straight-line on which we can move comfortably and easily; but it is a flexible-line, which may turn into any shape—zig-zag, curved, or any shape—which cannot be predicted and pre-determined. We may often face ups-and-downs and slow-and-fast in our life. People like palmist and fortune-tellers talk baseless things. They talk about fate and destiny and saying this, they encourage us to sit, wait, and do nonsense things, and then sleep and dream for success. No, this is a totally wrong-way of life. We must need to work and make efforts for what we want in our life. Therefore, for our development, we must utilize our total potential to our level best, and if possible, we should utilize it for development of others—for India and world, for one and all.

Thank You!

At the end of this book, I must say that I am thankful to you for reading this book. In modern age, people have very little time and interest for reading books, so really I am thankful to you. Now, you start listening to your inner feelings (little-voices arising within you) and make a habit to listen to them; and then move and act accordingly. Remember, only your own work and effort can make you creative, intelligent, developed and prosperous; and only your own heart and soul can guide you on the right path. Right path means the path of peace, awareness, science, creativity, prosperity and development.

At the end of this book, once again I strongly feel to say to every common man and especially to the youth of India that— do your best for India, only then we can change India!

All the best! God bless you!

✌

Compliments

अर्चना दत्ता (मुखोपाध्याय)
राष्ट्रपति के विशेष कार्याधिकारी (जन सम्पर्क)
Archana Datta
(Mukhopadhyay)
OSD (PR) to the President

राष्ट्रपति सचिवालय,
राष्ट्रपति भवन,
नई दिल्ली - 110004
President's Secretariat,
Rashtrapati Bhavan,
New Delhi - 110004

May 08, 2012

Dear Abhay Bahadur Singh,

This is to acknowledge with thanks the receipt of your letter 4th May, 2012, enclosing a book "How to Develop One & All" addressed to the Hon'ble President. The Hon'ble President sends her greetings to you and wishes you success in your literary endeavors.

With regards,

Yours sincerely,

(Archana Datta)

Shri Abhay Bahadur Singh
Ashoka Park Colony, Qtr. No.P 58/5
Kancharapalem (PO)
Visakhapatnam – 530 008
Andhra Pradesh, India

Tel. : 011-23016535(Direct), 23015321 Extn 4322, Fax 23794498, E-mail-osdad@rb.nic.in

Dr. Kiran Bedi
INDIAN POLICE SERVICE

Office Add :
56, Basement, Uday Park
New Delhi - 110 049 (INDIA)
Tel. : +91-11-47100700

Dated : August 03, 2012

To,

Abhay B. Singh
Ashoka park, Q. No. P58/5
PO- Kancharapalem
Visakhapatnam
A.P PIN- 530008

Dear Mr Singh,

May I take this opportunity to thank you for sending me the book **How to Develop One and All.** This is really a good attempt under your guidance & I respect your work.

With Warm Regards,

(KIRAN BEDI)

E-mail kiranbedioffice@gmail.com

Website www.kiranbedi.com

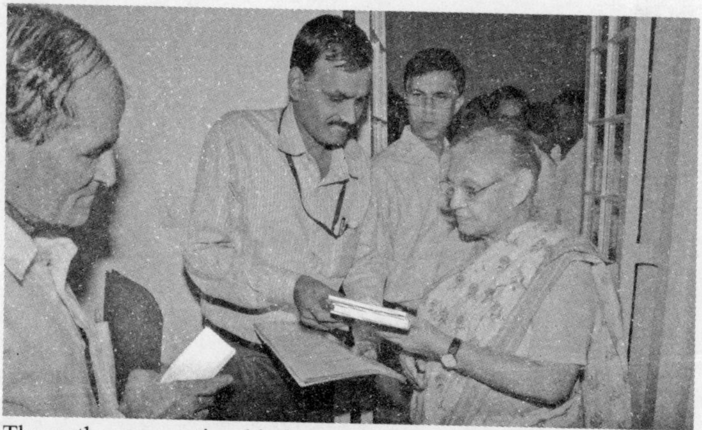

The author presenting his books and Synopsis of 'Yes! We Can Change India' to Mrs. Sheila Dikshit, Ex-Chief Minister of Delhi, and sharing a few words with her.